Smarter Execution

FT Prentice Hall
FINANCIAL TIMES

In an increasingly competitive world, it's quality of thinking that gives an edge – an idea that opens new doors, a technique that solves a problem, or an insight that simply makes sense of it all. The more you know, the smarter and faster you can go

That's why we work with the best minds in business, management and finance to bring cutting-edge thinking and best learning practice to a global market.

Under a range of leading imprints, including *Financial Times Prentice Hall*, we create world-class print publications and electronic products bringing our readers knowledge, skills and understanding, which can be applied whether studying or at work.

To find out more about Pearson Education publications, or tell us about the books you'd like to find, you can visit us at
www.pearsoned.co.uk

PEARSON
Education

Smarter Execution

Seven steps to getting results

Xavier Gilbert, Bettina Büchel and Rhoda Davidson

FT Prentice Hall
FINANCIAL TIMES

An imprint of **Pearson Education**

Harlow, England • London • New York • Boston • San Francisco • Toronto
Sydney • Tokyo • Singapore • Hong Kong • Seoul • Taipei • New Delhi
Cape Town • Madrid • Mexico City • Amsterdam • Munich • Paris • Milan

PEARSON EDUCATION LIMITED

Edinburgh Gate
Harlow CM20 2JE
Tel: +44 (0)1279 623623
Fax: +44 (0)1279 431059
Website: www.pearsoned.co.uk

First published in Great Britain in 2008
© Xavier Gilbert, Bettina Büchel and Rhoda Davidson 2008

The right of Xavier Gilbert, Bettina Büchel and Rhoda Davidson to be identified as authors of this work has been asserted by them in accordance with the Copyright, Designs and Patents Act 1988.

ISBN: 978-0-273-70931-2

British Library Cataloguing-in-Publication Data
A catalogue record for this book is available from the British Library

Library of Congress Cataloging-in-Publication Data
A catalog record for this book is available from the Library of Congress

Transferred to Digital Print on Demand 2011

Typeset in 10/13.5pt Gilliard by 30
Printed and bound in Great Britain by
CPI Antony Rowe, Chippenham and Eastbourne
The publisher's policy is to use paper manufactured from sustainable forests.

Contents

Prologue

The following is based on a true story.

IT IS SPRING 2005 and Richard Sparks can hardly believe his luck. His company, United Plastics, a petrochemical business based in the UK, has picked him to lead a major growth initiative. His boss has just given him his new brief: launch Siliflex, a promising new product range of polymer coatings, to customers in the American and European housing construction industry.[1] Sparks feels like he has won the lottery.

Sparks has been working for six years as the head of R&D for the Extrusion Coating business unit of United Plastics. He spotted the potential of Siliflex more than a year ago, and flagged it a couple of times to his boss. Over the years, Sparks has worked with more than 200 companies in the construction industry: he is sure Siliflex will be a hit. It had better be: there's a lot riding on it – for the company and for Sparks himself.

The Siliflex launch is critical to United Plastics, and Sparks will report directly to Manfred Manheim, a member of the Executive Board. Just thinking about the direct reporting line to Manheim makes Sparks queasy with apprehension. He finds himself pacing his office, his nerves on edge. He wakens at night, planning how to lead the Siliflex launch. There is no doubt about it: this is his big chance to prove himself. He can hardly wait to meet the team of six people Human Resources has handpicked from marketing, engineering, IT and R&D. With this high performance team, Sparks is sure he can deliver; he is opening a door to a new life.

Fast forward two years: It is now April 2007 and Sparks' team have missed the product launch date. There have been four major delays, and more minor delays than he can count. The project is already five months

---

[1] Name of the company and the characters have been disguised.

behind schedule – almost half a year. The product specifications have changed three times. Sparks sits hunched over his desk, asking himself over and over again 'What has gone wrong?' The same thought keeps coming back to him, 'If only the team had spent more time with potential customers early on in the initiative.' To make matters worse, the team put together the original plan with no input from the software developer. This added another chunk of time. Just yesterday one of his team members called him with more bad news: the pigment project, the next critical step, will be delayed for two more weeks. How could this have happened?

In his darkest moments, Sparks knows that no matter how many delays they overcome, they still have no contract with a major construction company. Not one. Sparks berates himself, 'We should have put a sales person on the team. If we don't find a sales person who believes in the product, a real product champion, we will never succeed.'

The team seemed so promising at the start of the initiative. Sparks is ashamed of how it has turned out. Three people on the team are doing just about everything. Two are only days away from burn-out. The other two team members can't help: which isn't their fault. They tried their best, but they just don't have the right skills. The place on the team reserved for a technical expert is still vacant.

Back at the start of the initiative, Sparks' sponsor from the Executive Board, Manheim, met with him every week. He went out of his way to find additional equipment for the team. But now the emails from him are intermittent. Each is more clipped and terse than the one before. The last one read: 'The Board needs an explanation of the further delay. Get back to me by Friday.'

As Sparks reads and rereads the brief email from Manheim, he can feel the pressure tightening in his chest. Time is running out on the initiative – and on him. Sparks knows that he just needs to get the product launched and book some orders. Nothing more. It sounds so simple. He stares at the computer screen and thinks, 'If only I had known more about execution at the start of the initiative.' What is he supposed to say to the Executive Board? 'Sorry, I never imagined how difficult it would be.'

Back in 2005, in the early days of the Siliflex project, he picked up a couple of books on execution at the airport. They pointed out over and over how important execution was, but they did not really show him what to do. Right now, his team doesn't need to work harder – they have already tried that. They need to work smarter.

Smarter not harder

Richard Sparks is not alone. Statistics on the low success rate of strategic initiatives abound and they are all uniformly disturbing. One recent survey of business-performance initiatives shows that only 38 per cent were either 'completely successful' or 'mostly successful' in delivering short-term results. Only 30 per cent were either 'completely successful' or 'mostly successful' in delivering sustainable results.[2]

As with Richard Sparks, the success or failure of a strategic initiative will make or break many careers. The statistics are stark. But it doesn't have to be this way. This book is about strategic initiatives like the one led by Richard Sparks. But it is not about the *what*, or even the *why* of such initiatives – there are lots of books on those topics. This is a book about the *how* of execution: how you can ensure that your strategic initiatives deliver on time and with the desired results. No one is saying that it isn't hard work. But it's a lot harder if you don't do it right. Of course, some people have to learn the hard way. They have to stand on the brink of disaster and seize victory from the jaws of defeat. If you are one of those people, then this book probably isn't for you. If you want the desperate grunt and groan of a burnt-out team working around the clock to hit an impossible deadline, then you will have to do it the hard way. But if you are looking for a roadmap to strategic success, then you have come to the right place. This is a book about how to execute a strategic initiative from start to finish – to achieve not just partial success but real success. It is about something we call smart execution. Interested? Read on.

---

[2] *Organizing for Successful Change Management: A McKinsey Quarterly Survey*, June 2006.

About the authors

XAVIER GILBERT is Professor of Strategy and holds the LEGO Chair in International Business Dynamics at IMD. He has also held various managerial responsibilities at IMD, such as being in charge of a financial turnaround in the early 1990s, and as IT Director. He is particularly involved in project-based learning initiatives, helping management teams develop and execute critical projects, as well as enhancing their managerial and leadership capabilities.

As a consultant, Xavier works with senior teams to help them focus their strategies on action and results.

BETTINA BÜCHEL is Professor of Strategy and Organization at IMD. She directs public and in-company programs and helps management teams implement their strategic change projects. Her current research topics include strategy implementation, new business development, strategic alliances and change management.

As a consultant, Bettina works with companies throughout Europe and Asia to facilitate their strategic change processes.

RHODA DAVIDSON is a Program Manager at IMD. She works with a wide range of multinational companies and IMD to design and deliver tailored programs that solve key business problems. She also actively supports post-program implementation to convert learning into business results.

Before joining IMD she worked at McKinsey & Company. She has a doctorate from Oxford University.

Acknowledgements

FIRST WE WOULD LIKE to thank the managers we have been working with over the years and with whom we have learned about the challenges of strategy execution. We want to thank them for entrusting us with their most critical initiatives, for giving us feedback on what worked and what didn't, for sharing their experience, for arguing with us and for thinking with us, for challenging us, for inspiring us. They taught us that, when it comes to execution, being an effective leader and being an effective manager are just the same.

We also want to thank Des Dearlove and Stuart Crainer for their advice and help in making our 'brilliant thoughts' actually legible. And we want to thank Liz Gooster for her patience and support when our own execution capabilities were not at their highest.

Finally, we owe a big thank-you to our families who have been the early victims of our adventure: the Gilberts – Cornelia, Clara and Hannah; the Raub-Büchels – Steffen, Julian and Aline; and the Davidsons – Graeme, Lara and Eliot.

Thank you,
Xavier, Bettina, Rhoda
September 2007

Introduction

You want it. We had it.

THE NOTICE WAS POSTED on a Japanese electronics shop: 'You Want It. We Had It.' It was nothing more than a slip-of-the-sign, a Japanese storekeeper who needed at least one more class in English translation. Yet, we'd suggest that all of us can learn a great deal about managing strategic initiatives by thinking about that sign. We have seen many companies come up with a great idea – a dazzling new product idea or an alluring new service – only to find that, despite the fact that the marketplace was hoping and waiting for such an idea, the ability to bring the idea to life was lost in mismanagement.

This is why execution is such a hot concept right now in B-schools and executive suites. And this is precisely why, despite all the talk about the importance of getting things done, so many strategic initiatives are fodder for case studies about failing companies.

Yet, it can be done. Some companies are remarkably successful at transforming ideas into reality. Consider James Dyson. Here's a business leader who knows the distinct difference between hot air and *hot* air! Dyson is a British entrepreneur who looked at the 100-year-old design of the basic household vacuum cleaner and thought it was time to reinvent a machine already owned by millions of people worldwide. His idea was to design a vacuum cleaner that one could see in operation, with floor dirt being sucked up and spun with immense centrifugal force in such a way that the dirt was split from the air and directed to a bagless chamber for disposal. Dyson's idea didn't rest idly in his mind; it didn't languish in his company's research and development lab; it didn't jam up or fall apart in the manufacturing process – and it certainly didn't get lost in translation when marketing took the idea to prospective customers. Steve Hamm reports in *BusinessWeek* (2 July 2007) that 'Dyson Appliances Ltd ... has the leading vacuum cleaner brand in the U.S., Britain, and Japan, with annual revenues topping $1 billion.'

According to the magazine, Dyson and his team are now planning to reinvent the hand dryer, the kind you see all the time in office and restaurant lavatories. The 'Dyson Airblade' will whisk your wet hands dry using an air jet that runs at 400 miles per hour. It's not just an idea whose time has come; it's an idea that is going, moving, selling. When you dry your hands with an Airblade, they are instantly dry. We're betting that Dyson Appliances will see their latest strategic initiative achieve results equal to or surpassing that of their vacuum cleaner line. And we're betting that it's because Dyson knows how to convert what's in his mind into something that can be bought in the marketplace; the company knows how to separate hot air – idle talk or lame action tied to a great idea – into an observable, measurable strategic initiative.

Tried and through

For companies, it's dangerous in today's marketplace to sit on one's laurels. The great commercial successes of the past are all either in accounts receivable, received or spent. Thus, many companies are looking for ways to boost the execution of their strategy. Everything around them is changing and they see it as unlikely that the same product or service line can work forever – rightly so. But some find themselves prisoners of their success. They have become so focused on what works for them that all they know is how to refine it. Others are prisoners of their problems. They are so focused on fixing them that they don't question whether there might be a better way to proceed altogether.

Whether they need to reinvent themselves, or to achieve a significant performance improvement, they find that they cannot do so with their usual approaches. Even if you try harder, more of the same will not produce different results. Something else must be done, outside the organization mainstream. It is not optional. It is not nice to have. Outside the organization mainstream, there is hidden potential that is not tapped.

Yet, although it's tempting to bank on what's tried and true, the probability is that strategic initiatives of the past – even if overwhelmingly successful – are not sustainable in tomorrow's workplace. Managers want to stick with tried and true when, in fact, they are sticking with something that's tried and through. Yet, most organizations have a very hard time addressing any opportunity that is outside their mainstream. They have been designed for efficiency. They consist of specialized silos that mind their own business, have their own resources and rely on their established knowledge. It is very difficult for them, if not impossible, to go beyond doing the same things they have been doing, time and again.

We're talking about the coffee shop that treads on and on while Howard Schultz invents and mobilizes the Starbucks phenomenon. We're talking about the clothing manufacturers whose web is woven with the same old styles that generate yawning sales while Amancio Ortega opens up a Zara store in La Coruña, Spain, to sell fashions in a whole new way. Now Inditex with 100 or more operating units has 1,000 stores in 31 countries. Inditex makes it a point to search the world for the styles young people want and then convert those trends into a product line – fast. We're talking about the UK supermarket Tesco and its chairman, Ian MacLaurin, who in the 1980s and 1990s (that's right, decades ago) started positioning the company for the savvy customer who wanted both quality and good pricing. Tesco now has some 900 stores in a collection of countries – but it's more than a *place*. Tesco has also become the world's largest *Internet* grocer.[1]

Such companies simply don't know how to plod. Why? Because, unlike their competitors, they do not worship efficiency as an end. Yes, they're efficient, but they're much more than just that. They're also willing to take new paths. Their competitors – those let's-just-be-efficient organizations – never allocate resources to focus seriously on anything that is not mainstream for them. The plodders love to operate with tidy silos, but you cannot see the big picture from silos. Even the central functions, for example, have difficulty integrating a local perspective into their central solutions. And new opportunities, beyond the mainstream, require new, non-standard knowledge. Merely efficient organizations are condemned to do more of the same, better and better, until it becomes irrelevant. Thus, the plodders really don't speak the language (or even understand the concept) of strategic initiatives. Strategic initiatives are designed to stop doing only more of the same. That's the whole point of them. Strategic initiatives are the way to work outside mainstream thinking, and outside mainstream organizations. Yet, before you can bring a strategic initiative to life, you have to know precisely what one is.

Beyond the mainstream

Companies like Dyson and Inditex don't mind keeping their business on a mainstream road; they're just far more likely than their competitors to either steer the company on to a new road – or build a road, if one doesn't exist.

---

[1] Information extracted from book research done by David Stauffer, used with permission (http://www.staufferbury.com/).

This is because Starbucks and Tesco see a value in strategic initiatives that their competitors do not. What do they see? First, strategic initiatives are a way to put focused attention, across the organization, on critical, leap-forward opportunities that are outside mainstream thinking and that cannot be addressed by the mainstream organization. These opportunities are vital for all companies. They are expected to have a major impact on the future of the company, in the short term or in the long term. Strategic initiatives have three characteristics: they involve a break with the status quo; they combine more than one functional view; and they are aimed at achieving something that has not been done before.

Taking these in turn: first, they are:

◆ A way to work outside the organization mainstream
◆ A flexible way to get an organization to focus on critical opportunities
◆ A way to deliver specified outcomes within a specified period of time.

Second, strategic initiatives take a cross-organization perspective.

◆ They bring together issues from across the organization: the whole company is at stake.
◆ They are meant to implement new ways of running the business across the organization: the whole company – and its customers – must benefit.
◆ They bring together teams, capabilities and resources from across the organization: the whole organization is mobilized.

Third, strategic initiatives are meant to develop on the go the new knowledge they require.

◆ They venture on to unknown territory; only how to execute the first steps is known.
◆ They require fast prototyping, fast experimenting, fast learning – in a continuous learning process.
◆ They progress in an agile way, flexibly rerouting execution to take most advantage from the learning.

Yet, a strategic initiative is not some magic elixir. It cannot rejuvenate or regenerate an organization that is half asleep because it is lulled into a false sense of security by the melodies of its own past success. In other words, strategic initiatives involve an element of change – and, with it, risk. Always. If they did not, then they would not be worth their salt. Let's face it: when you start down a new road (or build one), you could be steering your company into a swamp or off a cliff. Strategic initiatives can and do fail. But it's far better to understand a bit about how and why they fail and get back on track, than to recoil from the fright of trying something new.

Here's the stark, sad reality we have observed in dozens of companies: strategic initiatives fail mainly because they are executed as if they were just more of the same. It really is as simple as that. We have looked at more than 50 strategic project teams and talked with more than 300 executives to try to understand why the execution of strategic initiatives failed so often. We have identified *seven challenges* that many executives just fail to recognize when they launch a strategic initiative within an organization that is essentially focused on doing more of the same as effectively as possible.

These seven challenges are:

1 Focus first

Often, companies don't have clear strategic priorities. This reflects an unfocused strategy. It can range from a series of vague and ambiguous slogans that could apply to practically any company in any industry – 'We aim to be the world's best producer of (fill the blank space)' – to a series of financial goals with no mention of customers, products or services – 'Our strategy is to reach €1 billion sales revenue by 2010'. These slogans are probably good enough when the real strategy is to do just more of the same. We have seen many senior teams struggle and debate when asked what their three key strategic priorities are. Under these circumstances, *any* opportunity that passes by could be 'strategic'. And any initiative can be shown to have strategic impact. But new priorities will soon pop up and the initiative will be quietly forgotten.

Because of this undeveloped strategic thinking, many companies don't realize at the outset the extent to which their strategic initiatives will take them into unknown territory. Their feasibility is not carefully assessed. This is particularly true when the completion of initiatives extends beyond a few months and uncertainty follows. In the middle of execution, the expected outcome turns out to be irrelevant and the initiative has run out of resources.

This bad selection of strategic initiatives can often be linked to the fact that the senior management team is not seriously involved in the process. Parochial interests will prevail, instead of the overview perspective that should exist at the top. Initiatives are likely to be local issues, pet projects of little consequence, or even make-do projects. They will not get resources and the process will be an exercise in frustration.

2 Pick the best possible team

A sub-optimal team is a frequent cause of execution failure. The consequences are easy to imagine. What is surprising, however, is how frequently inadequate teams are assembled. Many companies have become accustomed to working with legacy teams that are good enough just to do more of the same.

All too often, teams are formed in an opportunistic manner comprised of people who are 'available' and thus make easy candidates. There is no opportunity to think seriously about the skills and capabilities specifically required by the initiative. The probability that this haphazard process will result in a strong team is close to zero. And that's the kiss of death, right from the start, to your initiative.

The importance of certain roles around the team is often underestimated. A case in point is the sponsor role. It is easily seen as occasional representation of top management. But without substantial, continuous senior management support, strategic initiatives soon lack the leadership and guidance they require.

Two other frequent team issues are time and performance management. Typically, people are assigned to a new strategic initiative team on top of an already demanding job or set of assigned tasks. Nobody asks how this is going to work – and it cannot work. Typically also, when people are assigned to an initiative, they take along their performance-assessment criteria. But these criteria don't always work for the initiative. Sometimes, they are even in pure contradiction to the execution of the initiative.

3 Set the course

Many initiatives address issues that are poorly understood. Their expected outcomes are fuzzy, and their main execution steps are nebulous. Worse, they make no room for inevitable context changes during execution. In other words, their scopes have been insufficiently thought out. Many companies are just not used to addressing non-mainstream issues. It is easy to conceive how this can undermine the execution of their strategic initiatives.

The logic to be followed is obviously not 'rocket science': Where are we? Where do we want to go? And how do we want to go there? But the rigorous thinking through this simple logic is often skipped. One main reason is the remarkable ability of some senior managers to issue fuzzy directions, particularly when they expect someone else, lower in the organization, to sort it out in due time. Later, in the middle of execution, confusion prevails and becomes deadly.

Time and again, we have seen strategic initiative teams unable to answer themselves these few simple questions ahead of jumping into execution: What exactly is the problem to be resolved? How will it look when the problem is resolved? How do we get there, flexibly, so as to navigate through inevitable context changes?

4 Play to win

Strategic initiatives are like a high-level sport. They require an extra, sustained, winning spirit. Those involved, and the team in particular, are certainly committed to their everyday job. But the initiative comes on top. They must find in the initiative new motives to win. Very often, they don't; and, thus, the initiative doesn't take off. Exhortations to commit are greeted with 'Yes, but...' meaning 'I think that I see that you are excited, but I don't think that this initiative is for me....' Result (and, no surprise): execution flounders.

The reason for the 'Yes, but...' is that the motives necessary for people to commit are simply ignored as frivolous and irrelevant. Many executives believe that the compelling logic of their strategic initiative, and the discipline of the troops, should be enough to get the job done. Well, actually, people also need strong personal motives to make the extra effort and win what still looks like someone else's battle. And this simple human need is routinely ignored. In such circumstances, for sure, there is little reason for enough people to commit and, as a result, there's insufficient energy to move the initiative ahead.

5 Think it through

Two equally dangerous temptations affect execution. One is to plan everything in full detail – right down to the tiniest detail – as if execution was to take place in a fully predictable context. With some chance the initiative might be completed, but the outcome will be irrelevant. The other temptation, because the detailed plans have turned out to be unreliable, is to improvise and hope for the best. The first steps might work fine, and then all degenerates to unplanned, unsynchronized chaos. Both attempts are typical habits from more-of-the-same execution – where they are of small consequence anyway.

It is a challenge to develop new habits suited to uncertain contexts. At any point in the execution of a strategic initiative, the team may only commit to its next few steps. Beyond, it needs to keep its options open until further information is gathered to decide more reliably. But these next few steps, that are to be executed in a foreseeable future, require to be thought through in full detail, thoroughly, leaving no stone unturned. They must be rehearsed mentally. In other words, all alternative actions must be reviewed, tried, challenged, like in a flight simulator. Developing the habit of mental rehearsal as a way to master uncertainty is a challenge when people are trained for routine.

There are three areas in executing a strategic initiative that particularly require this thorough advance thinking. They are often neglected but will inevitably catch up with a team if it tries to cut corners. One is thinking through the resources that will be required, with their owners – to secure their cooperation. The second is reviewing the key success factors of your next execution steps. The third is assessing, and being prepared for, their execution risks. You simply can't improvise these kinds of things, as we'll discuss later in this book.

6 Get all aboard

Without organization support, execution of a strategic initiative will never deliver its expected outcome. This is not an issue in more-of-the-same execution where it's all done according to well-rehearsed routines. But for a strategic initiative, there are no routines that apply. The challenge is that most parts of the organization don't even expect to be called on.

It starts with the visible absence of senior management who all get back to their preferred occupation as soon as the initiative has been launched. In such cases, the strategic initiative will be declassified immediately in everyone's mind as a low priority. This can also happen when the senior management team is perceived as not being totally aligned to support it. The effect is guaranteed to be disastrous.

Typically, those on the receiving end of the changes imposed by the initiative have not been brought into the loop. The silo mindset that prevails in many organizations means that, when you have a job to do, you just do it – without having to check with anyone else whether it might also make sense for them. The technical execution of the new process could be perfect, but it will never be applied because people don't see its benefits for them. The result is a waste of resources and many people across the organization who have lost faith in any strategic initiative from that point forward.

Similarly, many a strategic initiative demands the cooperation from various parts of the organization to provide resources or know-how. If they are also out of the loop and don't understand what the team is trying to accomplish, then it's unlikely they can be supportive. As a result, they often come off (unintentionally) as opposing the initiative. And if this is how they are perceived, this is also what they will end up doing.

Finally, the importance and diversity of public opinion is generally underestimated. Many people in the organization have a view on the initiative, justified or not. They also have influence, audiences and networks that can impact on the initiative. If, instead of being on board, where they stand becomes a permanent question mark, much energy will be wasted – energy that could help a company make a critical strategic initiative happen.

7 Follow through

For strategic initiatives, the lack of follow-through is a guarantee of failure. It is like navigating without a compass. You don't know where you are. You don't know where you have been nor how to improve. You lose faith in the whole trip getting anyone anywhere. This is what happens when you don't follow execution through to its full completion. Granted, in more-of-the-same execution, this is not particularly dramatic. The machine keeps on turning, more or less on schedule and on budget. Not much you can do about it anyway...

One of the activities in follow-through is progress reviews. In too many companies (especially the plodders) progress reviews are run as detective investigations: what did happen and who is the culprit? Those who are being reviewed dislike the inquiry process, which can seem like finger-pointing. Those following up avoid it because it seems that they are assuming the role of distrustful micromanagers. Team members will use whatever energy they have left to look for another assignment.

This is absolutely not what strategic initiatives need. Follow-through is all about keeping the course, but also learning on the go to keep improving the execution of subsequent steps and maintaining execution energy. The purpose and value of follow-through need to be taught and heralded. There is nothing in it that needs to be threatening. In fact, all should soon discover that they cannot perform at a high level without it. Indeed, plodding companies often fail to execute simply because few are motivated to learn how to move further, faster.

Seven insights

There is a large body of knowledge on project management. There are innumerable books and articles. There are methodologies and manuals. There are courses and certifications. For sure, this should help to execute strategic initiatives! Yet, we have observed that the same problems keep coming back to haunt companies. We believe this is not because the tools and techniques are unknown or misunderstood. Rather, we think that most failures – especially those tied to strategic initiatives – occur because managers are unaware of the extent to which these seven challenges require their personal attention before, during and after the start of executing a new initiative. That's why we wrote this book.

Our obsession is with simplicity and practicality. We have no ambition to be exhaustive, yet we do believe that focusing your attention on those seven challenges can help you win your strategic-initiative battles. We have advanced seven challenges that threaten the execution of strategic initiatives. We thus propose seven insights into these problematic areas. These insights are, in the main, a lot of common sense, but what we're doing is focusing on what we see as the most critical execution areas, the ones that separate those who think strategically but too often fail to *act* strategically. To some extent, our insights are about what to do in these seven areas. But please be assured: we will not provide you with extensive to-do lists. Instead, we will convince you that, if you follow the advice we share here, you will move much more assuredly towards the successful execution of a strategic initiative.

Our seven insights have one underlying *how* in common: the fate of execution is in *how* people in your company work with each other. Are you hands-on or are you hierarchical? Are you listening or are you telling? Are you close to the front line or are you looking somewhere else? Are you building on the ideas of others or do you know better? Thus, do not be surprised if this book sometimes provides the same feeling as those times when a wise counsellor placed his hand on your shoulder to proffer sage advice in a low-key yet emphatic way. There are many explanations of how companies like Tesco and Starbucks and Dyson succeed. But we've seen companies with equally great ideas stumble and fall. We don't want you and your company to be one of them.

Thus, you have our permission to read this book in a unique way: start anywhere. If you are focusing now on a strategic initiative, you are either about to begin its execution or have already started. Our seven insights are your paths to finding the best way to avoid failure. We trust that each chapter heading will attract you, based on your own priorities, to the best place for you to start reading. However, we have provided a simple map to get you started.

Our seven insights have a 'red thread.' We believe there is one insight that you should keep in mind *no matter where you are* in the journey of executing a strategic initiative. We've made that the fourth chapter of this book, right between the three chapters that discuss things you should focus upon before launching a strategic initiative and the three closing chapters that discuss things you must think about while in the actual stage of execution. Thus, you may, simply by looking at the following graphic, select the chapter that most compels your interest. So, begin anywhere: you can't make a mistake in terms of where you start your reading.

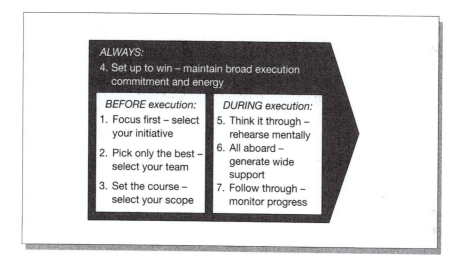

As you might guess, all seven insights are closely related to each other. After all, they all tie to the concept of making one strategic initiative come to life. But we divide them simply because it will help you to think of your seven challenges in helping your company succeed strategically. To our minds, the evidence is beyond any doubt. *You want it.* Every company we have observed or worked in wanted a strategic breakthrough, some exciting marketplace initiative, to elevate their status and bring them the rewards they craved. *We had it.* Too many of these very same companies were never able to convert bold ideas into bold actions. They had the great idea but, too often, stumbled, sometimes before the impact of the strategic initiative would even reach the marketplace. It does not have to be that way.

In the next chapter, we focus on the first of three insights you should think about before executing any strategic initiative. It has to do with focus. For we have learned that, if you don't know where you're going, most roads will turn out to be dead ends.

Focus first

YOU HAVE TO GO to Section 7 of their 2006 annual report, but there it is: Vallourec, a \$7.5 billion steelmaker based just outside Paris, reveals that it will team up with Sumitomo 'to jointly build and operate a seamless pipe mill in Brazil'. But it's further down the page that you see the word that attracted our immediate attention; the report states that 'This decision is perfectly in line with Vallourec's selective growth strategy, which essentially involves strengthening its presence in high added-value products while reinforcing the competitiveness of its production base.'[1]

In case you missed the word, we should repeat it with emphasis: *selective*. Vallourec's CEO, Pierre Verluca, and team realized the company needed to grow and change. According to one news report, Vallourec roots go back to nineteenth-century France. Surprisingly, the same report reveals that the company was a non-strategic amalgam of many unrelated businesses until the 1990s. The times were changing but, with its unimpressive growth, not so much for Vallourec. Even in 2000, all Vallourec factories were based in Europe.[2] Managers there might have talked about being a global player, but Vallourec was Euro-based, *sans l'ombre d'un doute*.

Verluca and his fellow executives had to confront what is, for us, the number one task facing a top management team. The major challenge that this CEO and many of his colleagues face is how to focus their organizations on the issues that are most critical. They have to concentrate organizational

---

[1] http://www.vallourec.fr/download.asp?murl=pub/rapports/2006-uk-1.pdf.
[2] 'Steel Beats the Odds', Carol Matlack, *BusinessWeek*, 3 May 2007
(http://www,businessweek.comglobalbiz/content/may2007/gb20070503_869191.htm).

energy on the tasks that will provide the most competitive and bottom-line impact. This is not only for immediate impact, but also to prepare the company for a future that seldom can be seen clearly or predicted with any confidence or certainty. Nonetheless, if the leaders of a company are doing their job, they have to be *selective* and they have to focus everyone on where the company needs to go. In Vallourec's case, the company sorted through and sorted out a mélange of businesses and zeroed in on two distinct lines: steel pipes designed for drilling oil and for use in power plants. The company is focused, and its 18,000 plus employees are moving in a new (and very profitable) direction.

What's the matter?

The purpose of strategic initiatives is to focus the execution of your strategy on issues that really matter. Sure, there are lots of things that need to be done. In a high-tech company making medical devices, after a lot of discussion on their strategy, we asked the top team what they believed their top strategic priorities were. We tried to stop them after they had already listed 15, but the CEO still had a few more that he believed were absolutely critical. No organization can work effectively on 15-plus priorities. No organization can work effectively unless there are but *a few* widely understood priorities. Your strategic initiatives are meant to deliver against these priorities – nothing else.

Your challenge is to select strategic initiatives that have impact on addressing your priorities. But it is also to ensure that these strategic initiatives are achievable without creating an unbearable stretch for your organization. A watch manufacturer, after all, cannot simply decide one day to become an automotive manufacturer. Impact and achievability are your two selection criteria. They sound straightforward, but they are, in fact, difficult to implement. They reflect many diverse factors that need to be combined. But there is no formula. It rests on executive judgment.

Your strategic priorities will be driven by the key building blocks of your competitive formula. Surprisingly, many companies are not totally clear on their competitive formula, on what makes their strategy tick. It is helpful to be able to explain it in a few highlight points that are easy to remember. Your competitive formula relies on four building blocks:

Your target markets, your target customers

Most companies take it for granted that they know their customers. In our experience, this is often decidedly *not* the case. We have seen proposed initiatives inadvertently shift markets, targeting out-of-scope customers, while missing those prime customers they should be serving.

Target markets and customers need to be described precisely. They are not whoever walks by. The most critical question is what does 'perceived value' mean for your target customers? What are they really willing, or unwilling, to pay for?

Your offer

Your offer is difficult to separate from your target customers. Together, they constitute the 'customer experience', what a customer experiences when buying and using your products and services.

Many companies offer great products and ruin the customer experience with unreliable delivery and impersonal service. Or their products have features and enhancements that customers are just not interested in paying for.

Your business system

Your business system connects all the activities that need to be performed to take your offer from the design labs to your target customers (this is also called activity system or extended value chain). You are never alone in performing the activities in your business system. You may license patents or outsource production and logistics. You may employ OEMs or special distribution channels. Keep in mind that your business-system fellows are competing with you for a share of the final customer's money. Selecting them is one of your most critical decisions. You want to keep them substitutable. And you want to make yourself irreplaceable in the customer's eye. This is not always possible, and compromises are often necessary.

Your economic model

Your economic model describes how you make money as a result of the above choices. Your bottom line could be driven by your ability to charge a price premium because of your differentiation advantage or by your volume of business because of your competitiveness on price. It is possible to make money with either approach. Competing for differentiation, or competing for overall price advantage, requires different markets, different offers and different business systems.

Often executives are not clear about what matters most in their strategy. In a survey conducted in companies planning to launch strategic initiatives, we found that about 30 per cent of the senior managers were not clear whether volume or differentiation was their most important bottom-line driver.

In any case, a characteristic that is common to all economic models is that you need to be the lowest-cost player in your market category. We have often heard the excuse that there was a cost penalty to being an industry leader; but we also volley back with this rhetorical question: what is the purpose of being an industry leader if you end up making *less* money?

Focusing on strategic priorities

Your strategic priorities will necessarily address the building blocks of your competitive formula, either one at a time or in some combination. Your strategic initiatives concern specific projects to deliver against your priorities.

◆ **Improving your customer focus**
   Developing a better understanding of your customers' business needs or developing new markets

◆ **Improving your offer**
   Developing new products and services or improving the fit between your offer and your target customers

◆ **Improving your business system**
   Fixing some business-system activities, improving the coordination across activities, adding or removing activities

These priorities all pursue the same purpose: to make your economic model more productive. This is one way in which you can measure the impact of your strategic priorities. So how do you begin to narrow down all that your company could or might do and arrive at a short list of true strategic priorities?

Consider the economic impact. After listing your options, assess their economic value creation, in essence, their net operating profit minus the cost of the capital employed. A practical way to arrive at that figure is to calculate the net present value (NPV) of the net cash flows generated by the initiative over its lifetime. This could give the impression of a fairly exact result. But the longer the period of time over which execution will extend, the more it is loaded with uncertainty. A positive figure at the bottom of the spreadsheet, however, will be surprisingly reassuring.

Typically, for example, the economics of large master-data or supply-chain initiatives are very difficult to prove conclusively. Consultants provide magic figures of savings on procurement or on working capital that, like heavenly promises, are listened to with awe. But, in practice, it is difficult to establish a figure for the overall investment as well as for the benefits. The cost of not going ahead seems more compelling than the uncertain return.

And the further you are looking into the future, the more elusive your calculations become. Ranking comparable initiatives according to the economic value they will create if successful will give a sense of where resources should be allocated. But, overall, executive judgement is still required, even when you are presented appetizing figures.

Balance the short term and the long term. While the economic impact is, of course, important, you also need to look at the timing of this economic impact. This is not only because a distant economic impact carries more uncertainty: it is also because you want to maintain your fitness in a constantly changing competitive context.

You should want strategic impact over different time horizons. We suggest three different levels with three different time horizons. (1) You want to make sure that your competitive formula works now as it should, (2) you want to make sure that your competitive formula remains effective as the environment evolves, and (3) you want to work on your competitive formula of the future.

1 Fixing your competitive formula

These initiatives are meant to bring your competitive formula back to speed, to fix it when it has deteriorated or in response to an unanticipated change. Or they are meant to quickly grab low-hanging fruit. They are reactive.

◆ You improve your focus on your target markets because they have evolved and you have ended up serving marginal customers who do not fit with the rest of your competitive formula.

◆ You improve your offer because some of its aspects no longer satisfy your target customers. Functionalities they expect are now missing or have lost their edge.

◆ You fix your business system because it has developed flaws that undermine your customers' experience. In many instances, when you refocus on your target customers and restore the leading edge of your offer, you will also find that your business system needs fixing. For example, your channels no longer serve your target customers as they should. Or your supply chain is in need of urgent streamlining to serve your target customers effectively against the competition.

These performance improvements focus on fixing what already exists. They rarely provide a significant competitive advantage. Their purpose is often to catch up with what your most successful competitors are doing. When they do make a difference, the improvements are often quite easy for a good competitor to match. Improvements of this kind can be described as 'necessary but not sufficient'.

The results of your fix initiatives thus need to be captured in a relatively short time-span. If you find that you need to spend years over them, you probably have a bigger problem than just fixing. If you need to fix your target markets and your offer at the same time, you are probably not looking at a fix initiative. In this category, bottom-line results should show up within 6–18 months.

2 Evolving your competitive formula

In the foreseeable future, some of the trends in your competitive environment will evolve in a more or less predictable manner. You need to maintain the fitness of your competitive formula through these extrapolative changes. Proactively and incrementally, these evolve initiatives will keep your competitive formula in tune with new opportunities and risks resulting from environment changes.

◆ You address a new target market with your current offer and with minor adjustments to your business system. This could be in response to the view that your current target market will not yield the growth that you need.

◆ You renew significantly your offer to your target market, with small adjustments to your business system. Indeed, you might have concluded that your current offer has become obsolete. Or you may have in mind additions to your offer that your target customers have not yet become aware of as a future need.

◆ You reconfigure your business system while your target customers and your offer remain the same. For example, you may want to implement a direct-sales channel that you believe should gradually replace a significant share of your indirect channels: this will help you retain all your current target customers.

Evolve initiatives generally provide competitive advantages to those who implement them first. They do not require a lot of insight. But if you move fast enough and have a full solution – that is, a target market, an offer and, most importantly, a business system that work well with each other – then your advantage may be more difficult for your competitors to match because it involves a lot of details that have to work well together.

Nespresso's response when lower-price alternatives to its espresso-coffee system (coffee capsule plus proprietary machine) arrived on the market was an example of an evolve initiative. Instead of responding with cheap systems, or with systems targeted on different markets, or even with a range of cheaper coffee capsules, Nespresso believed that there was a growing up-market that they essentially already owned. An initiative was launched to add new features to its classy Nespresso Club membership and a new line of design machines was launched. If Nespresso had not clearly stated its ownership of the lucrative up-market segment, or had confused its best customers about where it really stood, surely someone else would have taken its place.

Evolve initiatives will have a medium-term bottom-line impact – in, say, six months to three years. This time-span makes their successful completion more uncertain. You may want to split them into a sequence of execution steps. In this way, you only need to commit resources to the initial ones. The learning from these initial steps will help you decide how to shape the subsequent steps.

3 Transforming your competitive formula

The purpose of these initiatives is to shape your future, rather than let someone else shape it for you. They are meant to reshape your competitive environment by imposing a breakpoint with a new competitive formula that works best for you.

◆ Over time, your target markets will be significantly reconfigured and will develop new expectations. You have to define these new markets because there is no market research that will tell you what they will be and what they will need.

◆ Similarly, technologies will keep pushing the limits of products and services and you will have to develop new offers from scratch. Some of these technologies are probably not even in your labs yet. Again, no market research will tell you what they are.

◆ Of course, the way of conducting business will also change. Given the rate at which some economies are developing, supply chains are likely to change fundamentally, and growth and volume will require your presence in new marketplaces.

As you can see, you and your company have no choice but to enter these new territories. Your business context will get there, with or without you. If you don't shape that context yourself, someone else will do it for you and, in a few years, you will be struggling to catch up again.

The time-frame for turning your transform initiatives into bottom-line results is likely to be 18 months to five years, depending upon your business. In some industries, such as consumer electronics, it could be even shorter. In other industries, it can be longer. These longer time-frames definitely create uncertainty, and this is why many companies hesitate to launch transform initiatives.

But again, splitting them into smaller steps will give you a chance to learn your way into your future. Transform initiatives require a lot of experimenting. They must start from a relatively familiar territory (much like the mountain climber who secures three solid holds before moving her fourth limb to a new position). Progressively, these experiments will converge towards a transformed competitive formula by building on the learning of the previous steps. Launching a one-step transform initiative, on the promise of success in three to five years down the road, is a sure recipe for disaster.

Selection of the fittest

One philosopher put it this way: 'Nothing is more dangerous than an idea, when it's the only one we have.' We concur, especially when it comes to strategic initiatives. You probably want to have a range of initiatives, all the time, on your strategy roadmap, addressing different time-frames – some fix initiatives, some evolve initiatives and at least one transform initiative. Of course, much depends on the scope and complexity of your business. What we don't want you to forget is this important point: top executives are paid, first and foremost, to select the direction for the corporation. You need variety but you also need selectivity. No oil tycoon ever succeeded by telling his work crews to drill anytime, anywhere, anyplace.

Having only fix initiatives is unlikely to be sustainable. For sure, you become great at fixing, but that's all you will ever end up doing. Concurrent evolve and transform initiatives also need to be part of your roadmap. Otherwise, chances are that you will fix your competitive formula in a way that eliminates all degrees of freedom for shaping your future. Having only a transform initiative would also be of concern.

As a result, assessing the relative strategic impact of your proposed initiatives requires a fair amount of executive judgement. This is typically an area where applying the collective wisdom of a well-functioning executive team will help decide which initiatives would matter most. Once you have selected the strategic initiatives (your wish list, if you will) that you *might* pursue, you still have to assess the feasibility of your proposed strategic initiatives. A strategic initiative could theoretically matter from the strategy roadmap perspective and still make little sense because its feasibility would be quite a stretch for your organization.

Let us share with you such a case. A company manufacturing chip assembly equipment was keen to launch a generation of machines based on a new technology. A strategic initiative was launched to bring this new machine to market fast enough to preempt competition. Eighteen months later, the engineers were still struggling with perfecting the technology. The company had also discovered that this new technology only made sense for market segments that it had never served before. Finally, to be able to sell the machine at a price that had a chance to win customers, it was determined that manufacturing would have to be moved to Asia. On paper, the strategic impact was great. Practically, it all evaporated when the true costs of bringing the machine to market were assessed.

This company is not a unique case. Many initiatives are launched on promises that cannot be delivered and on assumptions that are only verified when it is already too late. An early-on assessment of the feasibility of the initiatives on your wish list will allow you to focus your resources where you have a higher probability of winning. Different factors can influence the complexity and feasibility of your initiatives.

Does the initiative have a manageable scope? Many strategic initiatives are first expressed as broad ideas, and this is absolutely normal in a first instance. Here are some examples from companies we have worked with:

- Establishing systems and processes to share innovations and thereby boost internal growth
- Improving the offer to customers buying special grades
- Developing best-practice HR processes for a customer-oriented organization
- Reducing the business-system complexity by removing unprofitable and non-strategic products and by standardizing packaging configurations.

Probably, the executives who proposed these initiatives had a particular scope in mind. Yet, they come across to others as fairly open. Eager and ambitious execution teams are likely to interpret such initiatives with an ultra-wide-angle lens.

The scope of a proposed initiative can be assessed by how much it tries to achieve at once: how many target markets it proposes to address; how many products and services it will cover; how many business system activities it will touch upon and the number and strength of competitors it will impact. Point: *the broader the scope, the higher the complexity and the lower the feasibility.* A broad scope is tempting because of its wider impact, but it also increases the execution risks. A focused scope, of course, achieves less, but it is more feasible and, more importantly, delivers results faster.

To increase the feasibility of a broad-scope initiative, you need to explore whether and how its scope can be made initially more focused. Then, step by step, the scope can be extended building on the knowledge acquired in previous steps:

- Targeting fewer market segments, for example, by starting with one or two pilot markets before rolling out across more
- Targeting a narrow part of the offer by focusing on a limited number of product attributes and leaving more for later releases
- Touching fewer activities along the business system by leaving the remaining ones for later runs.

Progressively broadening the scope, from known territories into unknown ones, will allow your execution teams to build knowledge in realistic instalments. Feasibility will be higher – and risk will be lower – than when you commit resources massively, all at once, to a complex scope.

Are necessary resources fully available? In some organizations, gathering resources from across silos can be 'mission impossible'. This is the reason why many initiatives are launched without verifying that the necessary capabilities and resources will be available. It would just take forever. And the fact that they exist somewhere in the organization makes people believe that they will be available eventually.

The availability of people with the required capabilities is always a bottle-neck when starting an initiative. Assigning people to strategic initiatives means that they will no longer be able to perform some of the tasks to which they are already assigned. We have observed many times that this simple 'human arithmetic' seems to be ignored. Eventually, everyone becomes overloaded and execution staggers.

The complexity of getting resources and people from different parts of the organization is also often grossly underestimated. Strategic initiatives are generally launched with little lead time, while the operating plans for the rest of the organization are set in concrete. Resources do exist, but they will not be available when needed. Everything is soon delayed. The windows of opportunity that had justified the initiative will be missed. Even with the best intentions, such a musical-chairs effect across the organization of re-prioritizing resources can create chaos. People often shy away from looking at it systematically. Rather than facing the reality of scarcity, they prefer to ignore the bottlenecks and to hope for the best: 'It will work out in due time,' these managers say. Well, in our experience, it won't.

We have also seen companies that believed that they had the capabilities and resources and, in fact, did not. Technology promises are a frequent case in point. Or local conditions cause some surprises. For example, the complexity of integrating legacy information-technology systems is often underestimated. Sometimes the missing capabilities can be developed or acquired, but some will remain out of reach within the time-frame of execution. Too little will be delivered – and much too late.

Facing this reality and its inescapable consequences will simply improve the feasibility of your initiatives. Perhaps it will lead to lowering the ambitions, but it will avoid costly failures at a later stage. Also, breaking resource-hungry initiatives into smaller steps will allow you to identify the required resources in a more informed way. Execution steps can then be scheduled taking into account the availability of the required resources.

How much change is manageable? Most people resent change. We tend to respond to it as we do to an illness, going in sequence through the classic (and much written about) psychological stages of denial, anger, bargaining, depression and acceptance.[3] Real change can be a long journey, and often people stop somewhere in the middle.

---

[3] This squence is known as Kübler-Ross Grief Cycle. It was initially developed to describe how patients respond to their condition.

Steering the change process is, of course, an integral part of executing a strategic initiative. There are some more or less objective measures tied to understanding change complexity: the size of the gap to be closed, the degree of urgency, the number of people involved, the sensitivity of the change and the speed of the change. These are useful to help you get a first assessment. But they don't necessarily convince those who are most affected.

It is *perceived* change that will matter most. Senior executives are not necessarily the best informed on these perceptions. Many throughout the organization will see the initiative as an unwelcome disturbance to their normal operations. Many will ask why they must forego a present state that is perhaps not great, but tolerable, for the promise of a better but uncertain future. For many, a better but uncertain future isn't a very attractive proposition – unless the 'platform' of the existing business is burning.

To think about how major change will be perceived throughout the organization, you need to look at precedents. Ask: What has been the experience with previous strategic initiatives? It will be used as a reference to assess the initiative at hand. Abandoned initiatives, failed initiatives and painful initiatives will increase the execution complexity. It's rare, but in some organizations change has become habitual and has acquired a reasonable reputation because it was worth it. However, in most cases, people resist change.

In fact, what these points show is that the emotional impact of an initiative can very easily become an additional factor of complexity for its execution. You may believe that your business logic is totally compelling. You may have the best set of PowerPoint® slides ever to communicate it. You may legitimately call for more organization discipline until you are literally red in the face. And yet, people won't move.

What is the time span for the initiative? The longer the time-span within which an initiative will deliver its promises, the higher the uncertainty that it will actually deliver. This is not only because a long initiative is more difficult to orchestrate: it is also because, when it does deliver (*if* it delivers), its promises will have become irrelevant because of context changes.

Fix initiatives are designed for a known and stable context. They just need to be executed very fast so that their underlying assumptions remain stable. Their relatively modest impact doesn't justify taking duration risks. Evolve initiatives are launched on the basis of the assumed trends in the competitive environment. If they are not executed rapidly, the window of opportunity will pass. If evolve initiatives cannot be executed rapidly, they must be split into several sequential steps. Before launching a step and committing resources to it, the assumptions on which it rests can be verified. And there is still a chance to steer the initiative so that it remains relevant – or even to stop it if evolution is no longer realistic.

Transform initiatives, by design (and by contrast), strive on uncertainty. How an industry segment will change in the future is really up for grabs. What is reliably certain is that someone will shape every industry's future and that others will have to respond by following or flagging. Transform initiatives require a substantial commitment, but, in fact, they find their way into the future through trial and error. They start with many trial initiatives on known territories to learn what works. Then, they push further, focusing on what works best and committing more resources to it so that all involved can learn more. Finally, they commit wholeheartedly to a chosen competitive formula that has now a good chance of working.

Sounds like a daunting proposition, right? Well, it is. Yet, the approach is not as risky as it may seem. While always pushing the limits, transform initiatives are close to known territory (as long as watchmakers don't try to build cars). In a rational transformation, managers will still have the resources to try an alternative path if one doesn't work for them. In truth, such transformations are less risky for those who initiate the change than for competitors who have to respond to it.

The bottom line is that what is most risky is to make an all-out commitment to a long path leading to a very uncertain future. The probability of achieving nothing of significance three years down the road would be extremely high, at which point there would be no resources left to try an alternative way. Yet, this is what many companies do.

Have you measured 'the familiarity gap'? Assessing the overall feasibility of your proposed initiatives clearly doesn't result from a mathematical average. Again, it is a matter of executive judgement: bringing together a large number of mostly qualitative factors into one final assessment. You need a range of strategic initiatives and you must be selective in which ones you pursue.

We suggest that you also organize your initiatives according to the level of familiarity that your organization has with the factors of complexity that you have identified.[4] How much experience and knowledge is available in your organization to handle this complexity?

---

[4] See Lowell L. Bryan, 'Just-in-time stratgy for a turbulent world', *The McKinsey Quarterly* 2002, special edition: risk and resilience.

- Familiar initiatives are those with which you already have experience. There are identified factors of complexity, but you have managed such factors before.

- Partly familiar initiatives have factors of complexity that you haven't mastered yet. But you are confident that you *can* learn how to do it. The knowledge the change requires resides in some part of the organization or outside – and you can access it.

- Unfamiliar initiatives take you and the organization to completely unknown territory. There are many factors of complexity that you don't know whether you can master. There are even some factors of complexity that you don't know yet.

Which ways to go?

There are different ways to present an overview of your strategic initiatives and, not surprisingly, they have similarities. We propose to do it along the two dimensions of strategic impact and familiarity. The combination of these two dimensions provides a view of your strategic roadmap, and of the risks involved in following it. The economic value of the various initiatives, if successful, can be shown as a third dimension.

Figure 1.1 represents a strategy roadmap. All the initiatives on your strategy roadmap should have an expected, and decisive, strategic impact. Yet, in a survey we conducted with senior executives in several companies, we found that 20 per cent of their corporate initiatives were estimated to have only a low strategic impact or none at all. All strategic initiatives consume valuable management time, and all can add to a state of organizational indigestion. We suggest that anyone who has resources for such low-priority projects probably has too many resources. The excuse of quick-wins is sometimes invoked to justify them; we would argue that your quick-wins should always be tied to something that affects the future of the business.

See 'Example of a strategy roadmap' opposite, as an illustration of how a company mapped its way to repositioning itself.

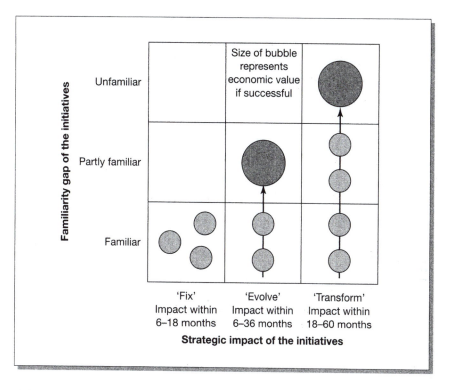

Figure 1.1 ◆ Strategy roadmap

Example of a strategy roadmap

A company we worked with had three main initiatives to support its overall strategy to move towards higher value-added activities:

◆ A *fix* one: to fix its production processes, which were placing the company at a cost and quality disadvantage

◆ A *develop* one: to take a leading position in one of its product categories, nicknamed the 'high-grades'

◆ And a *transform* one: to develop a new business area encompassing a range of services that were expected to become critical for customers, given the foreseeable increasing technological complexity of applying its products.

Its *develop* inititative and its *transform* initiative were in turn broken down into sequenced building blocks, allowing the company to learn its way from the familiar, to the partly familiar, and on to what was still unfamiliar territory.

Familiarity gap of the initiatives		'Fix' Impact within 6–18 months	'Evolve' Impact within 6–36 months	'Transform' Impact within 18–60 months
	Unfamiliar			Develop the service business
	Partly familiar		Establish world-class position in high-grades	Develop the diagnostic business
	Familiar	Complete production excellence initiative	Establish key account management	Pilot the diagnostic business in S-E Asia

Strategic impact of the initiatives

Source: Disguised case

Using the strategy roadmap, you should be able to see immediately whether there are gaps or oddly placed initiatives.

◆ If your initiatives are mostly on the fix side, are you really in such a crisis mode? Even if this is the case, a view of what you want to do next will ensure that your fix initiatives do not rule out future, better options.

◆ If they are clustered on the transform side, are you missing anything? Is your current business so perfectly designed? Or is it beyond rescue? Do you really want to bet the organization's future on a risky transformational effort?

◆ If they are mostly on the familiar side, are you sure that they will yield robust enough competitive advantages? Are you trying hard enough?

◆ If they are mostly on the unfamiliar side, in uncharted territories, what are your *real* chances of success?

◆ If they are clustered in one area of the chart, will you have the resources to perform them all? Even if they are clustered in the high-feasibility zone, they may really stretch your resources even though everyone knows what to do.

At this point, you may also ask how many strategic initiatives there should be on your strategy roadmap. If your impact and feasibility analyses have been realistic, you should end up with the right number of initiatives because their feasibility decreases when your resources get stretched. *Our experience is that a senior management team will be able to lead up to three, perhaps four, main strategic initiatives (or, rather, main clusters of strategic initiatives) at any one time.* Within these clusters, you may have a larger number of smaller initiatives; this is specifically the case with a transform initiative, one that will initially consist of numerous exploratory branches, as well as a more limited number of proof-of-concept and pilot initiatives.

For example, one company we worked with had three core clusters of strategic initiatives that were cascaded into 10 smaller, proof-of-concept initiatives. Out of these, six months later, some were regrouped and some were dropped. In the end, eight were vigorously pursued. Another company we worked with had two core strategic initiatives, one on cost reduction and one on internal growth. The internal-growth initiative consisted of two waves. Each wave included about 10 exploratory new-product or new-market initiatives. One year later, there were about half a dozen surviving initiatives on which the firm focused its resources.

Even fix initiatives may consist of a limited number of parallel work-streams all moving towards the same target. A commercial-excellence initiative we worked with consisted of three sub-initiatives: key accounts, pricing and value-adding services. Each sub-initiative was, in turn, split into a number of parallel work streams.

Your strategy roadmap is critical: place your options on this chart and then discuss – even debate – what commitment you can realistically make to each initiative. Most importantly, make sure that the strategic initiatives you map will get your company where you want it to be in the future, for there is one important factor that you need to think about as you weigh your strategic options. Whichever and how many initiatives you select will mean that you will not be able to allocate all your existing resources to current business operations. Unless you have the resources to completely fund and staff your strategic initiatives with *new, unallocated* funds and manpower, your ability to execute your initiatives will come from existing funds and manpower.

This is why you have to focus.

Your portfolio of strategic initiatives must be prepared and maintained at the highest level in your organization. Of course, there will be contributions from many people. Front-line people, close to everyday strategy execution, will suggest areas that require special corporate attention. Strategy departments will produce the data and the underlying analyses to select and position strategic initiatives. But, as we have seen, only the executive team has the overview, and can exercise the executive judgement, necessary to commit resources to the strategy roadmap. That is why, once the strategic-initiative roadmap has been plotted, much deliberation still remains to be done by the executive team via several questions that must be continuously addressed:

- Is our roadmap an accurate representation of where we want to be in the future? Is this where we want to apply our best resources?

- Do these initiatives make sense together? Do the pieces fit together? Do they provide a credible pathway?

- Is there anything that does not fit? Anything that feels out of place? Anything that gives an odd feeling in the guts? Or anything missing?

- And the most critical questions: Are we ready to commit to this roadmap? Are we ready to focus the organization's attention on it? Are we ready to follow it through?

'The task of management,' the German-born US diplomat, Henry Kissinger, observed, 'is to take people from where they are to where they have not been.'[5] We agree. But the move from where an organization is to where it needs to be is a task that must be a top priority of top executives. It must not be done cavalierly. It must not be done with abandon, with an attitude of 'try a lot of things and see what works'. More than anything, it must not be put off because there are too many options or factors to consider. Hamlet, after all, would have been a terrible CEO.

The future is a terrible thing to waste. We have but five words, then, to leave with you as you begin to select your strategic initiatives: focus, focus, focus, focus, focus.

---

5 'What is your managment style?', Thomas P. Sattler and Carol A. Doniek
(http://www.fitnessmanagement.com/FM/tmpl/genPage.asp?p=/information/articles
/libary/mgtmtrs/mgtmtrs1096.html).

2

Pick only the best

BMW IS ONE of the great automotive manufacturers, one that – along with Porsche and Ferrari – defines sleek and stylish European motoring. In September 2007, for the third consecutive year, the BMW Group was leading the automobile industry in the Dow Jones Sustainability World Index, reflecting its commitment to saving resources throughout its value chain. 'Communications and teamwork are the lifeblood of our business,' observes Dr Martin Rudolph, a project manager in the Information Technology section of BMW. 'We depend on these two factors in all aspects of our business – from our research laboratories, which aim to develop more environmentally friendly engineering, to the systems that we use to support our network of dealers.'[1]

Today's business world works in teams. And there is virtually no strategic initiative that can be performed without a combination of talents, levels, skills, nationalities, geographies and tenures. In an interview with the *European Business Forum,* famed management thinker Henry Mintzberg underscored the importance of teamwork by stressing the importance of team skills starting at the highest levels of any company: 'Real leadership is often more quiet than heroic. Any CEO who is worth his or her salt should be "living" teamwork.'[2]

---

[1] 'BMW Takes Employee Collaboration to New Heights with Communication Software', Microsoft (http:/whitepapers.techrepublic.com.com/casestudy.aspx?docid=274108) 2007.
[2] 'Henry Mintzberg', *European Business Forum Online* (http://ebfonline.com/Article.aspx?ExtraID-32).

To live teamwork, as Mintzberg puts it, you not only have to pick great people to work on your teams, you also have to create and encourage a system that leverages the power of individual workers and managers by teaming them *with others*. And when it comes to new strategic thrusts, you must get the best people on the teams that will matter most to your company's future.

Dream teams

The decision of whom to recruit to the team is vital for the success of any strategic initiative. The best team possible must be recruited. This doesn't just mean the best available team. It means the best *obtainable* team. The reason is obvious. With the best team you increase the odds that the initiative will succeed. However, there is another less obvious reason: who is assigned to the team is a message to the organization of how important this initiative is. And it is not just who is assigned that is important: it is also the care and attention in selecting these people. When the senior management team hand-picks the team leader and each of the team members is personally asked to join the team by one of the management team, then, right from the start, this raises the personal stakes for everyone involved.

Unfortunately, for most companies, recruiting the best obtainable team is a near impossible challenge. The best people are already totally occupied in running current operations. And as companies drive for increased productivity and attempt to run their business with as few managers as possible, these people are expected to take on more and more. So their agendas are already crammed.

What should you do? Assign the best people anyway and hope that miraculously they will manage to juggle their current commitments with yet another project? The risk for your strategic initiative is that the manager cannot devote enough time and energy to the team. The risk for your organization is that one of your best people becomes totally overworked, overstressed and burnt out. Don't go there.

The answer is to put in place human resource processes that treat assignments to strategic-initiative teams as a significant career-path assignment. In many companies, they are sadly treated instead as lacklustre career parentheses. Line managers must expect that their best people will be offered development opportunities such as working on strategic initiatives. How can your company achieve such a level of respect for teams tied to major strategic initiatives? We'd suggest that you think, hard, about three aspects in creating any team: making sure the team has a dedicated sponsor, selecting a team leader who inspires true teamwork, and attracting team members who want to win.

Sponsored talk

The meaning of 'sponsor' here is the person who provides resources and support for the initiative in exchange for deliverables. The senior management team is collectively responsible for the execution of strategic initiatives. However, practically, it makes sense to assign one person from the senior management team, or a person appointed by this team, to sponsor each initiative. This person, whom we call the initiative *sponsor*, is then accountable to the top team for results.

As mentioned above, without the clear support of the senior management team, the organization will not perceive the initiative as urgent or important. The initiative sponsor embodies this support. Choosing not to appoint a high-level sponsor is usually the kiss of death. One manager told us after an initiative, 'The strategic imperative for our initiative was provided by the Board and by our sponsor. They created a sense of urgency and expectation. The President also made it well known that the team's work was very important. Without this we could not have succeeded.'

How closely the sponsor chooses to be involved depends on factors such as the degree of risk of the initiative, the experience of the team leader, whether the initiative is a short sprint or a long distance, and so on. But to be most beneficial to the team, the sponsor needs to maintain some distance from the day-to-day trials of execution. Does that mean that she only plays a limited role? Not at all: the sponsor has a key role to play in each of the seven execution tasks on which we focus our insights.

Setting direction and priorities

When the team gets lost in the details, the sponsor is there to remind them of the link between the strategy and the initiative, providing the big picture context for the team's actions. The sponsor also has to take certain decisions on behalf of the team. For instance, decisions to go ahead at a major milestone, go and no-go decisions, decisions to replace team members or even the more fundamental decision to stop the initiative altogether.

Forming the team

The sponsor should have a say in the selection of the team leader with whom he will be working very closely throughout execution. Selecting individual team members, on the other hand, should be left to the team leader. But the sponsor has a role to play in making sure that the team is working effectively. The sponsor will probably also have to intervene to make sure that the team members have enough time available to work on the initiative.

Confirming the scope

The sponsor confirms the scope of the initiative with the team and the target levels that the team aims to achieve. Confirming the scope is a critical decision. This is when the pilot chart of the initiative is set. It will be the only way to know whether the team is on course, at any time, in the middle of execution.

Monitoring the execution energy

The energy level of the sponsor is contagious, like that of a sports coach spurring a team to higher performance. The sponsor demonstrates a high level of personal commitment during both formal review sessions and chance corridor meetings with team members. The sponsor must also be able to sense how the team is working.

Mentally rehearsing next steps with the team

The sponsor acts as a sparring partner to test out the team's thinking. He challenges their ideas, examines their assumptions, raises 'what if' questions, probes for contingency thinking. He is also ready to ask the naïve questions that the team has overlooked because they are too close to the action. He is constantly enquiring about major risks that might throw the initiative off-track and challenging the team on how they will deal with these risks.

Synchronizing tasks

The sponsor has an important role to play keeping the rest of the organization in tune with the strategic initiative. On a daily basis, the team is expected to manage this interface with the rest of the organization. But there may be some instances when high-level intervention from the sponsor helps. For instance, teams may have problems gaining timely access to services performed by other departments or functions.

The sponsor also needs to act as the team ambassador, to mobilize support and gain buy-in from influential stakeholders. Another role is to continuously maintain a positive buzz about the initiative. A positive reputation helps to turn the success flywheel and keeps the initiative at the top of the organization's mind.

Following through

The sponsor monitors progress until full completion of the initiative. This is the main purpose of follow-through. The sponsor cannot delegate this job. The sponsor also makes sure that the team learns from their experiences, so that execution keeps improving and so that the next moves are executed with a solid knowledge base.

Many executives shy away from this role, making excuses that they have other important things to do. But this is the key job of the sponsor, because he is ultimately responsible and accountable for the deliverables.

As you can see from the above, the job of the sponsor is hands-on, to say the least. Any sponsor thinking about all of these responsibilities should take out a pen and estimate how much it will take to ensure the success of the strategic initiative. This figure may come as a shock. Our estimate is that it takes, on average, one day a week. Yet, it's not just the time a sponsor spends on teamwork that's important; how the sponsor comes across matters equally.

Choosing the right sponsor is important. And yet, from our experience, this does not always happen. Sometimes companies make fundamentally bad choices. For instance, some sponsors are just not sure what they want from their initiative. One team told us, 'Whenever we discussed what to include or not include with our sponsor, he was so vague. Every time we tried to suggest excluding something from the scope, he told us that we should include it. He was just not willing to make his mind up either way.' Of course, at the outset of an initiative, the scope may not always be entirely clear but the overall objective has to be clear. It's not enough for a sponsor to say, 'I'll recognize it when I see it.'

Some sponsors unfortunately demote the role they have on a strategic-initiative team; they always seem to 'have more important things to do'. They see the occasional sponsoring of an initiative as unavoidable, but it is not what matters for them. A perceived lack of interest will not do much good for the team's motivation. One team told us, 'Our sponsor just took on a new job within the company. He is leading a major restructuring plan within one of the divisions. We have not seen him for six months.' Believe us, that strategic initiative will go nowhere fast.

What are the essential traits in a sponsor? Here's our view.

- The sponsor must have visible stakes in the success of the initiative. Failure cannot be an option and must have consequences for the sponsor, as it should have for the rest of the team. The team has to feel that they share the execution risks with their sponsor and that he is not going to point the finger at them if the initiative fails to deliver.

- The sponsor must be a credible role model in the organization in terms of his capabilities to lead and manage change. Selecting a sponsor with a controversial reputation, whether in terms of managerial character or track record, signals to the organization that either style or results don't matter.

- There is nothing wrong with a sponsor who has strong opinions on how to do the job, but he should also have the ability to keep an open mind on possible approaches. If the team finds that the sponsor is holding a gun to their heads to come up with the 'right answer', the team will probably comply. But they will also conclude that the initiative (and their efforts) were useless.

    One team we worked with was asked to evaluate the option of centralized or decentralized IT systems within their European operations. The head of Global IT, as the sponsor of the project, gave the team clear guidance. He expected the team only to build the case for centralized IT. The team resigned, realizing that the process was rigged and that both options would not get a fair hearing.

Some companies prefer to use a steering committee rather than a single sponsor. This can have some advantages. First, a high-level team can provide more political clout and amply demonstrates the commitment of senior management. Second, the team can obtain several different points of view and have access to several sparring partners when planning execution. Third, the team may get better access to resources when working with a group of sponsors.

But there are also major disadvantages. Often it can be hard enough booking appointments with one busy executive, let alone a whole group. Also, there is a tendency for everyone on the committee to be responsible and for nobody to be accountable for the outcome. We worked with a team that had two sponsors. Each one kept telling the team that the other sponsor had the decision-making power. In fact, they had strongly conflicting political agendas. They were using the team as a punching ball. The team leader resigned from the company. The initiative was in disarray until the approach was changed. When steering committees work well, it is a dream situation. But when they don't, it is misery for team members; they would probably be better off with no sponsor.

Lead to succeed

Recruiting a team leader is not a routine decision. The team leader is the pivotal role in any strategic initiative and has direct responsibility for its successful completion. Given this person's importance, senior management must be involved in the selection process to ensure the best choice and to signal the importance of the initiative to the organization.

It is worth pointing out that the role of the team leader is always somewhat ambiguous. The team leader is the team's manager for the purposes of the initiative. But, at the same time, the team members retain their straight-line reporting relationship to their line managers for their regular jobs. Thus, the team leader has limited formal authority over each team member. She is expected to run a mission-critical initiative with what amounts to a web of dotted-line relationships. You can immediately see that this is a challenge!

As with the team sponsor, the team leader has a role to play in each of the seven execution tasks on which we are focusing our insights.

Setting execution priorities

During execution, the team leader continually reminds the team of the ultimate destination and the priorities for reaching this destination on time. She has a strong grasp of the 'big-impact' details. These are the details that have far-reaching implications in relation to the big picture, for instance, a sub-project on the critical path or a key supplier whose cooperation is essential.

Forming the team

Senior management may have a point of view in suggesting who should be on the team. But at the end of the day it's the team leader's job to make the final selection. You cannot make a team leader accountable for a team that he has not selected himself.

Setting goals

The team leader will work with the team to propose the scope of the initiative. She will make sure that the problem to be addressed is fully understood. She will make sure that the team is aligned on the expected outcome of the initiative. With the team, she will define the main activities to be completed. She will make sure that these activities are sequenced in a way that ensures execution flexibility.

Sustaining the energy level

It is the team leader who sustains the energy of the team on an everyday basis. To do this he has to be in close contact with each team member and take a personal interest in what fires their energy. He needs to engage with them, sense their mood swings and be ready to rebuild them during times when they are down. Because he is in a good position to judge team members' performance, he is the first one to recognize high performance.

Rehearsing every execution step

The team leader carefully reviews every execution step with the team. She makes sure that each team member is prepared for what is coming up next. For every step, she sets intermediate goals so that it is easy to see when team members are running behind schedule or off-track. She is constantly looking ahead to pre-empt any risks that might throw the initiative off-track. She makes sure that the team has its resources lined up and contingency plans made.

Synchronizing team member efforts

There are many forces that can lead team members to diverge. The team leader keeps the team internally synchronized. He ensures that the sponsor is in the loop and agrees on the team's mode of operation. He also keeps the rest of the organization informed and involved so that the team can access resources, involve stakeholders and maintain the initiative buzz.

Following through

Follow-through is a critical task that the team leader shares with the sponsor. She constantly monitors progress and makes sure that the team members are realistic about their current position and what they have achieved. She is on the front line to maintain team momentum.

Given the role of the team leader, you can understand that their selection is not a routine decision. Substantial homework is required to find the right person. Again, there is probably a long list of leadership capabilities to look for, but here are the essential ones:

◆ Select a manager who has a reputation for getting things done. The individual should have:
  - Some project management track record
  - Some experience with change management
  - Some evidence of being able to influence without authority
  - Some experience with cross-silo work.

◆ She should be able to show visible personal commitment to the success of the team and each of the team members. She should:
  - Ensure team members' personal success rather than taking the limelight
  - Have contagious personal energy
  - Stand up for personal values and beliefs.

◆ The team leader must understand his own weaknesses and recognize how to compensate for them by including people on the team with complementary strengths.

Of course, team leaders work primarily with the members of their team. However, they must also work with the sponsor of the team. The boundary between the job of the sponsor and the job of the team leader is not a fixed one. It varies by agreement between the two of them. There is overlap, but there are also differences.

The difference in roles is important and useful. The sponsor definitely focuses on the big picture, where the initiative fits in the overall strategy. The team leader has to focus on everyday execution. The sponsor approves the pilot chart: the scope and the main execution steps. The team leader is in charge of the detailed execution of every step. The sponsor focuses on the forest, and the team leader on the trees. They cannot work without each other.

Taking advantage of slightly more distance from execution, the sponsor can also act to reset the team's direction, if needed. The team leader should be the usual guide for the team's work. If, for whatever reason, the team leader is taking the team off mark, the sponsor can intervene.

There is also overlap between the two roles. For example, the regular team meetings are normally run by the team leader. However, the sponsor may decide to attend some of them to get a feel for how the team is progressing. When mentally rehearsing the next execution steps, the sponsor may be present to challenge the thinking of the team. There are critical points when the presence of the sponsor is important to support the team leader by affirming the team leader's management.

The quality of the working relationship between the two is essential for execution. Any unusual tension will be immediately felt by the team, and its performance will inevitably suffer. The team leader needs to keep the sponsor thoroughly informed of what is going on in the team. The sponsor needs to act much like a sports coach, and, if this is done correctly, there is an equilibrium that the sponsor and the team leader will define together.

Recruit for energy

Putting together a high-performance team is never a decision to be outsourced to a third party, such as human resource representatives. They can help, but they don't have the in-depth knowledge to judge the capabilities required by the initiative. Often, they also lack the leverage to extract the best people from their current jobs.

Who, then, should choose team members? As mentioned at the start of this chapter, the personal involvement of senior management in team selection reinforces the level of importance of the initiative and the corporate agenda. It is also a good way for senior management to identify and develop talent. For instance, Visa International launches a small number of strategic initiatives each year that they use as a training ground for their up-and-coming managers. Once a manager has successfully operated as a team member, then he can expect to lead an initiative team in the coming years. Promotion to a senior position in the company requires the manager to have successfully led an initiative team.

However, the team leader is the person who has to work with these people on a daily basis and will be held accountable for getting each of the team members to execute. So, although senior management should have a say in who should join the team, the team leader should make the final decision. There's an interesting story that shows the importance of this point.

In April 2000, Chris Johnson, a 39-year-old American running Nestlé's business in Taiwan, received a phone call from his boss: he had been chosen to head up a major Nestlé initiative called the 'Globe Program'. The general goal of the programme was to transform Nestlé from a collection of independent fiefdoms into an integrated company showing a common face to customers and suppliers around the world.

At the first meeting with his new boss, the vice-president of finance and administration in Nestlé's head office in Vevey, he was handed the list of people on his team. Chris had already thought about his dream team – a small core of people located in one building with no reserved parking spots, only a few titles and high bonus potential. But he took the time to check the credentials of the people on the list. When he got a negative report on one potential team member, Chris became uncertain whether to include him or not. Given that the person had been promised a position on the team, Chris had to decide whether to disagree with his new boss. At this point, he decided that he would not appoint any team member that he had not chosen. He went as far as making it a condition for accepting the job. Because he would ultimately be responsible for the outcome of the initiative, he wanted to get started with the best possible team.[3]

People often ask us what is the 'perfect' size for a team? The magic number is seven. More people can also work with the core team during certain project phases. But seven seems to be the number of core team members that works best. With more than eight or nine people, team meetings become too long-winded and exhausting – it takes too long to listen to everyone's point of view. The other team members have mentally passed on to the next issue, and there is a strong risk that the team will splinter. With fewer than seven people, decisions can become almost too easy. There are not enough minds to challenge the consensus. Diversity of opinion is beneficial. You need enough people with diverse experiences and backgrounds so that the team as a whole can hear all sides of the story.

Seven is also a large enough number to include some diversity of expertise. The high complexity of strategic initiatives requires expertise across a number of areas. At the same time no one is an expert in everything. There is always someone who can ask the dumb questions in someone else's area of expertise.

Putting together the best team is more an art than a science. Obviously you want people with the right skills and expertise. However, there are other factors to take into account.

---

[3] *Nestlé's Globe Program (A): The Early Months*, Peter Killing, IMD Case 3-1334, 2005.

Keeping the strategic initiative in mind

Even before thinking about the potential team members, you need to construct a list of the most important aspects of the strategic initiative: the goals, the nature of the tasks, and the capabilities needed. Use this list as you start to assemble the team mentally to see how each individual fits and how you can justify their team seat.

◆ Which areas of technical expertise are required?
We worked with a new product development team that consisted entirely of team members from R&D. Without input from marketing and sales, this team was clueless about what the customer wanted. And without input from production, the team did not know if the new products could be manufactured profitably.

◆ What is the desired execution style?
Is this a change initiative? If so, the team members will have to deal with resistance from stakeholders. Or is this a development initiative such as a new product launch? In this case, the team needs creativity and out-of-the-box thinking. Or is the initiative politically complex? In this case, the team should have on board people who can negotiate and build on common ground between the various parties.

Respecting all stakeholders

It is essential that the team be able to represent the viewpoints of all the key stakeholders.

◆ For example, the future users of the initiative outcome should be the experts on how the current situation arose and on the most critical issues to be addressed.

◆ The future providers of resources should be the experts on the feasibility of any proposed approach.

How better to tap this expertise than to have them represented on the team?

Uniting members with team chemistry

Team chemistry is seldom taken into serious consideration when putting together the best team. People are expected to be grown-ups and to perform under any circumstances.

We worked with a team in which all the team members were out-and-out creative extroverts. Team meetings were extremely noisy and disorganized with everyone trying to convince everyone else about their latest brilliant idea. Not a single team member was prepared to listen. It was mayhem.

Team chemistry matters. As one execution leader told us, 'If people have a poor attitude, then it can spread like a virus.'

Utilizing diversity

Teams benefit from a certain amount of diversity. Here diversity refers to culture, gender, background, work experience or thinking style. Research shows that diverse global teams generally perform worse than homogeneous teams but can also perform much better if they are well managed.[4] Team diversity, within reasonable boundaries, produces creativity and innovation. But too much team diversity makes it difficult to reach closure and to find a working style that suits everyone.

So, in putting together the team, you should explore the thinking styles and personalities of potential team members. For instance, in any team it is useful to have a mix of profiles, such as those identified by the MBTI®[5] or the Diversity Icebreaker™.[6]

We suggest three dimensions along which diversity proves to be helpful in an initiative team:

◆ *Attending to both overview and details*
You need people who have overview capabilities: they can keep the big-picture perspective in mind. They help the team to prioritize the tasks. They prevent the team from getting lost in less relevant details. At the same time you also need people willing to immerse themselves in detailed planning.

◆ *Integrating doers and thinkers*
You also need a balance between individuals who have a tendency to reflect and those who have a tendency to act. If your team only has reflective people, then nothing will get done. On the other hand, with only doers, the team will not take the time to think through the right approach.

---

[4] 'Creating Value with Diverse Teams in Global Management', Joseph J.DiStefano and Martha L. Maznevski, *Organizational Dynamics*, 2000.
[5] *Myers-Briggs Type Indicator.*®
[6] *Diversity Icebreaker*™, Human Factors AS, Oslo, Norway.

◆ *Focusing on logical and emotional issues*
You will need some people on the team who have a genuine interest in people's motives. Rational people tend to believe that sound logic is automatically followed with action. You also need team members who will dare to ask questions such as, 'How will we sell this to our staff? Why should they want to go along with this plan?'

Encouraging complementarity

You should look for complementarity in the team, between the strengths of one team member and the weaknesses of another. For instance, we worked with a team in which the team leader had limited project management experience but this was balanced by having two experienced project managers on the team.

Putting attitude first

When selecting team members, you should always prioritize positive attitude over expertise. Lone experts are useless. You need people who can support each other and challenge each other. Big egos can do neither of the two. They are best left off the core team or included on a temporary basis.

Two time bombs

Now you have selected the best possible team. Everything looks good.
Watch out.
You may have two time bombs that could affect your team.

The time-availability time bomb

The first one is time availability. It is timed to burst out relatively fast. We have already alluded to it several times. When your team members are assigned to the initiative, they are still doing their normal job. What will they no longer be doing in that job to make room for the important work of the initiative?

It is generally a fair estimate that the initiative will require two to three days of their time per week. Two to three days is in the dangerous zone. At the outset, it is greeted with denial. People think that it is an exaggeration, and they believe that they are more productive than what was assumed. Many people do not want to imagine that they are unable to cope. So the issue is first swept under the carpet. But, inevitably, it will explode very soon. How could anyone fantasize that the best people in your company are still looking for something to do for close to 50 per cent of their time?

There is simply no alternative to being upfront with any potential team member and the team member's line manager regarding how much time she will need to devote to the initiative. If the organization has long experience with cross-organizational teams, then the team member can probably reach this agreement directly with her boss. In other cases the team leader or sponsor will need to secure an agreement. Some companies use a sign-off sheet that makes this type of agreement crystal clear. The following can perhaps illustrate the importance of all these points.

In 2003, a European chemical company launched a series of growth initiatives. At the start of these projects, the team leaders were formally assigned to spend 50 per cent of their time working on the initiative. The team members were assigned at 25 per cent. The Executive Committee communicated and agreed to this time allocation with the line managers of the team leaders and team members. Most of these project teams were virtual teams, team members spread around the globe, only meeting face-to-face four or five times a year.

Within a year it became clear that the time allocated to the initiatives was simply not enough. Most of the team members were so totally swallowed up by their day jobs that they were allocating very little time to the initiatives. The teams missed deadlines and did not reach their initial targets. Team leaders complained that team members showed almost no commitment and displayed little accountability for results. However, those few initiatives in which the team were working full time flourished and progressed as planned. As a result, in 2005, the Executive Committee renegotiated the team member commitments with their line managers. Where possible, all team leaders were assigned 100 per cent to the project and team members were assigned at 50 per cent.

The performance-management time bomb

This time bomb will generally take somewhat longer to explode. What is the problem under consideration? We recall meeting one manager who had just agreed to her bonus criteria with her line boss; all the paperwork was forwarded to HR. But she was later assigned to a special initiative team, actually reporting part-time to someone else! How was her performance to be assessed, by whom and according to which criteria?

Performance management processes often don't have the flexibility to integrate unplanned changes. And there is no process that can accommodate contradictory performance indicators.

As a team leader, you need to hold preliminary performance discussions with your team members so as to identify these issues as early as possible. Then, they have to be resolved on a case-by-case basis. Both the line boss and the team leader will have to work at it; the sponsor may even have to help. In some instances, the official process will have to be tweaked to take special cases into account. Sometimes it will even imply changes in the performance-management criteria in the home unit of a team member.

Companies that have a cross-organization team culture clearly have an advantage. Some, for example, have sensibly designed their objective-setting forms with a special section where a manager can add project work as the year unfolds. We recall a situation in one workplace that shows how this can be managed to maximum advantage.

In 2002, a large consumer goods company which had grown rapidly through a series of acquisitions launched a supply-chain initiative led by the corporate centre. The goal of the initiative was to reduce supply-chain complexity through SKU harmonization and packaging standardization at a local and regional level. The initiative was led by the head of group procurement and each of the local supply-chain directors was on the team. To encourage the local organizations to implement these supply-chain changes, the team leader gave each team member a generous budget to recruit expert resources or consultants.

By the end of 2003, the team leader was extremely disappointed. The local supply-chain managers had taken very few actions and the overall number of SKUs and packaging types had substantially increased rather than decreased. Most managers had not even spent the money he had given them on the initiative but had just added it to their own supply-chain budget.

As the head of group procurement tried to work out what had gone wrong, he found out that these local directors were rewarded based solely on the sales of their local organizations. Supply-chain measures were irrelevant. So, working through the CEO and HR, he managed to add the relevant supply-chain performance measures to their objectives. By the end of 2004, it was a different story. The number of SKUs was on the way down. Following a new wave of packaging standardization, the team leader estimated that the company had already saved €20 million and more savings were in the pipeline.

Creating a team

Attaining high team performance requires intensive social interaction, so when the team members first meet, the priority should be to build a supportive social context. Many people are fairly dependent on social acceptance to be able to perform. Fear of rejection is a natural reaction of people who meet for the first time. It can lead to some apparently irrational behaviours triggered by primal defence mechanisms. However, ordinarily, team members will unconsciously be testing whether the rest of the team accepts them. They will assess where they are in the pecking order, and who are the dominant team members.

It is important to monitor this encounter process so as to avoid certain team members taking positions vis-à-vis each other, positions that could subsequently damage team effectiveness. Two activities are vital in this regard.

Getting to know each other

To make the first team encounters as stress-free as possible and to build social connections, you should focus your first meetings around team building. There is nothing wrong with people introducing themselves or introducing each other. Some activities help lower people's guard. Some emphasize the need for team support. Other activities promote open communication. Games in which there are clear winners and losers are not very helpful at this stage.

There are many options, so there is no need to invest in expensive outdoor training. Simple activities such as walking in the forest or in the countryside are just as good at this early stage. Singing exercises, theatre acting, or drum playing exercises have also proved to be very effective with teams.

Establishing team norms

Team norms are extremely important. We do not see them as a nice-to-have option. They are a productivity tool. They are meant to allow the team members to focus safely on the work at hand and to avoid energy-wasting frustrations. They are decided by the team. Once they are decided, it is easier to point to them than to argue with a team member on what is proper behaviour. Team norms set the boundaries for what is expected behaviour, and what is unacceptable behaviour.

Team norms are under your responsibility, as are team members. Before you start work as a team, organize a session in which you set out some simple team norms about how you want to work together. There is no right or wrong answer for team norms, but every team member must be invited to contribute to the norms and the team has to agree on them. As a guideline, five or six norms are about the right number that people can remember.

Here are some of the topics that you could consider:

◆ Norms about the housekeeping aspects of teamwork, for example, roles, attendance, timeliness, preparedness, how to handle interruptions in the form of phone calls or emails

◆ Norms about behaviour during discussions, for example, respect for team members by not interrupting, sticking to the point, listening

◆ Norms about how the team will detect and resolve conflict (particularly important because these norms help team members to feel 'safe' about disagreeing with other team members)

◆ Norms about how the team will take decisions, for example, consensus, majority vote, team leader has the last say

◆ Norms about email etiquette, for example, keeping them short and sweet, highlighting their main points, banning political CCs.

Once you have agreed on your norms, post them where you regularly meet. You must agree on how you will police your norms. Specifically, you need to agree that whistle-blowing is safe. In some cases, you may agree on small penalties, such as a small donation to a charity. It is good practice at the end of each meeting to review what to watch out for during your next meeting.

As a team, you should periodically review your norms and update them. There may be some norms that have become second nature, so they can be taken off the list. But there may also be emerging issues that require new norms to regulate and improve the team process.

Perhaps the most important thing you can do as a leader to encourage teamwork as the best way to achieve success on a strategic initiative is to relate to all involved that the best corporations *think* as a team. Google's facility in Ireland was named in the 2007 list of the '100 Best Workplaces in

Europe'.[7] Google worldwide subscribes to 'ten golden rules' for enhancing the company's productivity. One of those rules has to do with the subject at hand, and when Google CEO Eric Schmidt talks about the importance of teamwork, here are the words he uses:[8]

> ***Strive to reach consensus.*** *Modern corporate mythology has the unique decision maker as hero. We adhere to the view that the 'many are smarter than the few,' and solicit a broad base of views before reaching any decision. At Google, the role of the manager is that of an aggregator of viewpoints, not the dictator of decisions. Building a consensus sometimes takes longer, but always produces a more committed team and better decisions.*

[7] '100 Best Workplaces in Europe 2007'
(http://www.greatplacetowork-europe.com/best/list-eu.htm).
[8] 'Google: Ten Golden Rules', Eric Schmidt and Hal Varian
(http://www.msnbc.msn.com/id/10296177/site/newsweek/).

3

Set the course

ELISABETH MARX and Steve Tappin, from the executive search firm, Heidrick & Struggles, could not be more blunt about it: 'Progression to a senior business role requires the ability to operate strategically: to develop a helicopter view and think in the long term.' Yet, they quickly amend this point of view; we suspect that's because they both know – having recruited dozens of high-powered corporate leaders – that *just* having a big vision of where a business needs to be is much like the football coach who only knows where the goal is located at his team's end of the field. That's not nearly enough. Finding the way to get your team to score is what top coaching jobs are all about.

Marx and Tappin add to their comments:

Yet strategic thinking isn't enough on its own: it needs to be complemented by a focus on operational results and the ability to switch easily from long-term to short-term thinking, from helicopter view to operational details, and from cost-saving to expansion mode. The flexibility to handle this potential paradox and deal with seemingly incompatible extremes is what characterises the top executives of the future.[1]

The first part of this book has been focused on the insights we have gained from watching dozens of highly competent managers who started to execute a

---

[1] 'Leadership – Managing paradox', Elisabeth Marx and Steve Tappin, *Management Today*, 1 September 2006
(http://www.managementtoday.co.uk/search/article/591704/the-mt-essays-40th-anniversary-leadership-managing-paradox/).

strategic initiative *without* being prepared for the job at hand. They remind us of sailors who leave port without a map (maybe even without a compass!).

Don't sail without...

Before you sail off on a transatlantic journey, you pull out the route charts. You mark where you are. You mark where you want to go. And you draw a tentative route, taking into account the weather forecasts, the currents, the seasonal prevailing winds, the desirable ports of call.

Scoping your initiative is exactly the same. It is an indispensable preliminary to a long execution journey. It draws the large-scale chart for executing your strategic initiative. From it, you will be able, in due time, to make sure that your smaller execution components all point in the right direction.

Before scoping, your strategic initiative is still a fairly general idea. People believe that they know what they want. But if you start questioning the main players, you realize that they have different interpretations of almost everything. They have different interpretations of the problems to be resolved. They have different interpretations of the expected outcome. And they have different interpretations of the in-between conditions.

The purpose of scoping is to set this general idea on the right course, to make it a tangible and executable undertaking. It sounds quite straightforward, and it is; but it takes time, which always challenges those with insufficient patience. Yet, be assured: the hours and days spent on scoping is time well used. Imagining that you can execute a strategy without thorough scoping is guaranteed trouble. We say this having seen many strategic initiatives sag or fail simply because the front-end thinking and preparation were sacrificed by impatient managers in too much of a hurry. Our files are filled with instances like this:

◆ Some companies jump straight into detailed execution planning, as if they were putting dozens of small-scale maps next to each other to chart a long-distance voyage. Soon, they no longer know where they are – or maybe even where they want to be.

◆ Sometimes, the scope of the initiative is left fuzzy. This is a sure recipe for 'scope creep'. People come up with new ideas and new demands. And the team constantly adjusts the scope of the initiative to respond to the latest suggestion. This is one of the deadliest enemies of execution. The team ends up chasing a moving target: complexity increases and the initiative is never completed. A precise scope helps the team decide whether the proposed changes make sense or whether they should be kept for 'release two'. And it helps the team be upfront with what will not be done.

◆ Sometimes, the scope of the initiative is too ambitious. This is generally the result of indecisiveness. People don't want to take the risk of leaving out something that might turn out to be important. So they leave it in. It is not less risky, but more risky. It is better to deliver something incomplete and then complete it, than to not deliver at all.

◆ Sometimes, the scope is embarrassingly narrow. This is generally the sign that the team has trimmed the initiative down to the scope of their ordinary jobs. It can be a reaction of people who are overloaded and try to be productive. Or it can be to minimize additional effort. In either case, it doesn't deserve to be called a strategic initiative.

Keep this always in mind: scoping is, first and foremost, for your team, the people who will actually have to make the strategic initiative not only happen but succeed. Sometimes, the scope of the initiative is handed over to the team as an operating manual. 'Just do it!' the manager exhorts. This is not a good approach. There are two reasons why the initiative scope must be shaped by the team.

◆ The first is that performing this task creates alignment among the team members. They have to agree on what the problem is, what the goals are, how to get there. These points have to be common decisions.

◆ The second is that scoping is the first important opportunity for the team to work as a team. Discussions to define the scope give the team ownership of the initiative. It becomes *their* scope and they are committed to its execution.

Some senior executives may be worried about ending up with a scope that has nothing to do with their original idea. As we will see, the risk is very low. There will be many opportunities for the sponsor to challenge the team's thinking and ensure that the scope that is finally approved is relevant.

In fact, many teams fear that they will make a mistake by selecting the 'wrong' scope and make top management unhappy. At this early stage, they typically have a limited understanding of the issue. So they turn to their sponsor for the 'right answer'. Precisely, the sponsor shouldn't have *the* answer. She should point out to the team that the very reason why they are on the team is to provide *their* answer. She should throw the ball back at them and challenge them for some push-back.

These initial discussions with the sponsor are important to help the team and the sponsor calibrate their expectations. The team should test and retest their views against the sponsor's views. They should debate these boundaries until both sides have established a common understanding. During these debates the sponsor can demonstrate her commitment and her style of interaction. As one sponsor told us, 'I like to walk around the subject more than once, to address the same questions more than once, from different angles.'

Three steps to set the course

You establish your point of departure.

You choose your point of destination.

You draw a route between the two.

Sounds simple. But these three steps, if done correctly, do not happen as a straight-line process. There are feedback loops between selecting the starting point, the ending point, and the route. There are different route options. There will be some trial and error in setting the course.

Deciding on the scope of your strategic initiative requires that you:

◆ Agree on the problem to be resolved by the initiative

◆ Agree on the expected outcome of the initiative

◆ Agree on the overall roadmap to get there, with some possible options along the way.

1 Agreeing on the problem to be resolved

Many initiatives are not clear on the problems that the team will address or the opportunity that the team will exploit. Often, encouraging team members to dig into the details of the current situation does not meet with enthusiastic approval. Frequently, you hear team members say, 'We know what the situation is; no need to waste time on this!' Typically these comments come from action-oriented managers who would much rather rush off to do something, in fact anything, rather than sit back and think.

But without understanding the departure point, you risk addressing the wrong issues and hence choosing the wrong scope. This section provides you with an approach to effectively capture a snapshot of the current situation that draws out the main problems that the initiative will resolve.

Find the root causes, not the symptoms

Teams often only look at the symptoms of the problem rather than getting down to the root causes of the problem. It is clear that just removing the symptoms will not resolve the problem.

We worked with a team who decided that their problem was their small size relative to the other players in the region. They identified potential acquisition targets among the smaller players in the region. The idea was that they would transfer their home best practices to the acquired companies and consolidate them. They launched an initiative to execute this strategy.

But upon closer examination, the initiative team realized that their home operations were actually extremely fragmented. There was no way they could even assemble a pool of best practices, let alone transfer them to the acquired companies.

They proposed to shift the scope of the initiative. Instead of making acquisitions, their suggestion was to unify best practices in the home operations first. Only then could they be reproduced when making acquisitions abroad.

The approach we propose to uncover the root causes of a problem is called the *fishbone diagram*, or the *cause-and-effect diagram*.[2] It is well known in quality management circles. The effect, or problem to be addressed, is written down at the head of the fishbone. The causes are progressively added along the bones, in the order in which they are identified (see Figure 3.1).

- The investigation starts with four main categories of possible causes, just to stimulate the imagination. Frequently used categories are people, processes, policies and equipment.

- Whenever a cause is proposed, the next question is: 'Why is that?', leading to another deeper cause. The 'Why?' question is repeated until the team runs out of usable answers.

- Some causes will appear with a higher frequency across branches: they are the most likely causes.

- The collective wisdom of the team is then used to prioritize the identified causes (for example, by sticking red dots next to those that are deemed most important). The most probable root causes are those at the top of the priority list.

---

2 The method was initially designed by Kaoru Ishikawa who pioneered quality management in Japan.

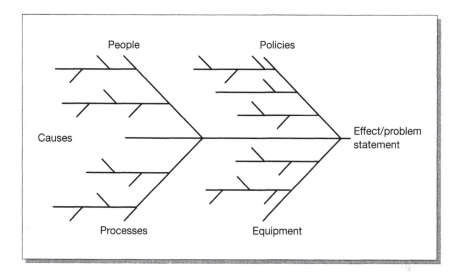

Figure 3.1 ◆ Fishbone diagram

The process is participative. The whole team can contribute ideas and ask 'Why?' There is no need to be an expert on most of the causes to propose possible deeper causes. And proposed causes should never be criticized, just written down on the fishbone. The collective wisdom normally takes care of the unlikely causes. The process also helps people focus on causes, rather than on people.

Identify existing knowledge and best practices

At the same time that you are identifying the root causes of the problem, it is important to find any relevant knowledge available to address this problem. Teams often fail to capitalize on previous initiatives that examined similar issues. Some sponsors even actively hide previous initiatives from the team, claiming that they want the team to start with a clean sheet. This is nice in theory, but in practice a good team is not unduly influenced by the past mistakes of others. In fact, just the opposite; they learn from these mistakes. So do your best to find out what has been done before.

It is also important to identify any best practice that could be relevant to addressing the problem. This can be inside or outside the company. There is no need to reinvent the wheel. Also, looking at how your problem has been resolved by a company in another industry can be a mind-opening opportunity.

Synthesize

At this point, your team may suffer from data overload. You should step back and work on the big picture. The question that the team should answer is: 'What are the three most critical issues that we need to address?' Three because, as the Pareto Principle suggests, chances are that they represent 80 per cent of the problem. And, as we will see, you should probably address these issues one at a time, anyway, to get execution feedback before moving on.

We find that it is helpful to draw a visual overview of the problem synthesis: for instance, a network diagram showing the location of the most critical issues, or a process-flow diagram highlighting the critical bottlenecks. A graphical view is useful because it helps the team converge and provides a centrepiece for discussions. As thinking evolves, the team can modify the overview picture to reflect this evolution and then use this graphical view with other people to test their thinking.

Get feedback on the problem

The final part of agreeing on the current situation is for the team to get feedback on their analysis. This validation exercise needs to be done at three levels – within the team, with stakeholders, and with the sponsor.

- First, you need to validate your own thinking. You need to list the assumptions or beliefs that have been made when synthesizing the key issues. Then, one by one, you need to challenge them. What have you taken for granted in your analysis? What facts and figures do you have to support your claims? For instance, if the team thinks that it is obvious that certain distribution channels are not working well, then, what is the evidence of this?

- Secondly, you need to get feedback on your diagram from your key stakeholders. Does the picture 'ring true'? Your stakeholders are primarily the future users of your initiative output: those who have the problem. They may not think that they do, but this also is feedback.

- Your stakeholders are also your providers of resources to execute the initiative. They certainly also have a perspective on how to address the issues that you have identified.

- Thirdly, you need to seek being challenged by your sponsor if you haven't yet done so. Explaining the whole picture to your sponsor, with words and sentences, is also a way to explain it to yourself. This mental rehearsal is, for you, an opportunity to verify your logic.

◆ A suggestion: when you have these discussions, try not to use slides; it is much more effective to use a diagram posted on the wall or drawn on a whiteboard.

Sponsors, a special note: if you don't challenge your team effectively at this critical point, you are going to leave behind a very disappointed group of people – at least if they are any good. An agreement on the problem to be addressed, between you and the team, is essential to move ahead from a solid foundation.

Try it out – get feedback – improve

This first step, agreeing on the problem to be resolved, should not be downplayed. You will hear people arguing that they can tell you immediately what the problem is. Perhaps your sponsor will do so. You will have team members who can't wait to get into action. It is very important that you take the necessary time to go systematically through the process and confirm, or not, the team's views. A poor definition of the problem to be resolved will follow you and drag you down all along.

That said, don't go to the other extreme that we have sometimes observed. This occurs when everything is a problem. 'Some people like to raise all possible problems to protect themselves, like a vaccination!' observed a leader we worked with. The process that we have suggested should help you out of that syndrome. Before the list of problems becomes unmanageable, synthesize, validate, get feedback and improve.

The whole process is in fact a classic *hypothesis-testing* one. Its cognitive effectiveness is well known. It consists in proposing hypotheses and confirming them through selective research. Some people fear that, in this way, they will miss important data; so they end up accumulating more data than they can handle and finish up in confusion.

As a team, you are now sharing a common view of the problem to be addressed. This view is in sync with the expectations of your most important stakeholders. It also has the support of your sponsor. Finally, you sense that this iterative process has helped to increase the personal commitment of each team member.

2 Agreeing on the expected outcome

The expected outcome that you were given as a mandate was probably as general as the initial problem definition itself. Your task is now to make it ambitious and achievable. How will it look when the problem has been resolved? As one project leader told us, 'Once we got together, we really forced ourselves to decide on the criteria of success and used this to drive the project.' This section provides you with some tips for how to do this.

Have a dream

This is not hype. If you don't have a dream, you will never start pushing the limits. Later, we will make sure with you that your dream is achievable. But now, it's time to have a dream.

Or rather, have a dream for the future users of the initiative outcome. If the initiative is looking at improving a business process, what do the front-line users of this process need to run their business even more effectively? If the initiative is about a new product, what would really make potential customers immediately switch to your product?

The process we suggest leverages team dynamics. It uses team interaction to push the envelope, by building on each other's ideas. The idea is, again, to quickly propose ideas, get feedback, and improve them. The process follows five steps.

Set the challenge

The challenge consists in a deliverable plus some constraints. The deliverable could be 'Design the ideal process to work with key accounts' or 'Design a service offer for our premium customers'.

The constraints have to do with the execution of the dream: for example, an implementation time frame, an overall cost, a technological limit.

Assemble enough collective wisdom

In addition to the initiative team, you should invite a diverse group of people: key stakeholder groups who have an opinion, topical experts who are familiar or not with the initiative issues, people who are known for being creative within the organization and people who are known as independent thinkers. Divide the people attending into groups of around four to five people.

Prototype

Ask the teams to brainstorm initially on the desired features that should be in their outcome. The normal rules of brainstorming apply: defer judgment, build on each other's ideas, and so forth. Writing individual ideas on Post-it® Notes is helpful because they can be moved around on the working space. They can be regrouped by category.

Some teams have difficulty not putting their final solution immediately on paper. But you should insist that you get feedback on the desired features first, before finalizing the output design.

Prototyping sessions of about one hour work well.

Get feedback and improve

Each prototyping session is immediately followed by a feedback session from the other groups. Feedback is also provided on Post-it® Notes. This should help the team whose prototype is being examined refrain from arguing in defence of its work. It also provides a written trace of the feedback directly on the workspace.

You may have three to five prototype-feedback iterations. As we said, the initial iterations should provide feedback on desired features. The later iterations can be on full visual representations of the prototype, like a process flow, or even a product model. In this process, it is possible to borrow good ideas from each other and to expand them.

Finalize

After enough iterations have been completed, each group presents its prototype. The other group members can assign 'points', in the form of sticky red dots, to specific features that they value in the prototype, or to the entire prototype, relative to the others.

At this stage, the initiative team can assemble one single prototype of the desired outcome, using the best features from all prototypes.

Make it tangible

Now you need to turn your dream into a tangible desired outcome. This doesn't mean compromise with your dream. But ultimately, you want an answer to the question: 'When it's all done, what evidence will show that our dream has come true?' Such evidence can be that the performance measures of a process have improved; that the sales or market-share figures of a new product have increased; or that a business unit has increased its economic-value creation.

Qualitative assessments are sometimes tempting, but must be avoided: a glass is always half-full and half-empty at the same time. Sometimes, you may believe that it is not possible to quantify the outcome. Intangible benefits also exist and are, by definition, hard to quantify. However, it is in your best interests to come up with an inventive solution if you want your results to be unquestionable. As one execution leader told us, 'I ask them to quantify things that they don't believe can be quantified.' See 'Imaginative measures of success' for an example of such measures.

Making your dream tangible requires demanding deadlines.[3] A dream without a deadline should instead be called a fantasy. A stretch deadline forces the team to coordinate more effectively, to learn faster and to focus on the highest priorities. As we will show later in this book, time is a critical driver of success in most initiatives. This overall execution deadline is vital, because it calibrates the entire execution plan.

Imaginative measures of success

A team located in the UK from a large European utility company was launching an initiative to, first, identify responsible procurement practices with their major UK contractors. Then, they were to transfer them to other markets within the company. This initiative was viewed as a good way to reduce exposure to third-party risk. The company's reputation could be at stake if any of their contractors behaved in an environmentally or ethically irresponsible manner.

The initiative would require the buy-in of many different stakeholders, including the UK legal department, UK procurement department and the Corporate & Social Responsibility (CSR) Council at the European level. At first it was hard to think of quantitative measures of success, but following a brainstorming session the team decided on:

- UK legal-department appraisal of the risk to the brand integrity before and after the project.

- Number of mentions of the issue of responsible procurement practices at the CSR Council during the year before the initiative and the year after the initiative.

- Corporate social responsibility rankings for the company made by NGOs before and after the initiative.

---

[3] See *A Dream With a Deadline*, Jacques Horovitz, Anne-V. Ohlsson, Prentice Hall Financial Times, 2007.

Don't be tempted to set the execution deadline by adding together the durations of each of the major phases in the initiative. Instead, look at the window of opportunity within your business environment. What is the deadline dictated by your competitive environment? How far behind the competition are you with respect to this initiative? Or how far ahead of the competition do you want to be? How long will it take them to react? What are the benefits of achieving an earlier result?

Get feedback on the expected outcome

Again, you must seek feedback from the same people with whom you validated your understanding of the problem to be resolved.

◆ Of course, the future users of your initiative outcome will certainly be interested. If you provide them with a *fait accompli* at the end of the initiative, when all the money has been spent, you run a clear risk that it will never be used. You need their involvement to allow you to prioritize the expected functionalities from the outset correctly. Discuss how you selected and prioritized this list and ask for feedback. Describe the measures of success and the specific targets that you have chosen. Find out whether they agree with these measures.

◆ The feedback from your providers of resources will also help you verify the feasibility of your ambitions. In addition, this is a way to give them an early warning that you are striving to achieve great things.

◆ Seeking feedback from your sponsor is also important at this stage, although you have probably done it all along. You need her agreement on your proposed outcome. And your sponsor will certainly want to use this opportunity to challenge your thinking and to verify that your dream is both ambitious and achievable.

Through this interactive process to define the expected outcome of the initiative, your team develops a common ownership of this outcome. Clearly, this would not happen if senior managers simply set down the initiative goals. Now, for the team, the expected outcome should no longer be 'their goal' but 'our goal'.

3 Agreeing the execution roadmap

Now you need to fill the gap between the problem to be resolved and the expected outcome. You need to select and sequence your main execution phases. At this stage we are only concerned with your overall route: the main execution phases, and not yet with detailed planning.

Sequence your execution phases

Execution phases require inputs and turn out deliverables. Inputs and deliverables provide the main logic for sequencing execution phases. The deliverable of phase A is an input to phase B. In principle, you need the product before you can sell it. Interestingly, there is one input and one deliverable that are easily taken for granted. The input is knowledge and the deliverable is money.

Frontload knowledge development

We worked with a team that was asked to launch a new technique for fireproofing plastics. The team conducted many customer interviews to establish the demand for the new product. They were on the verge of marketing the product, as part of their launch plan in a selected pilot market. They had not verified one key hypothesis: that the technology worked. At this point they were told by the R&D expert that the product just did not work.

The lesson is: for each of your main execution phases, make a list of all the input knowledge that its execution requires. Don't take anything for granted. Then, make sure that that knowledge is explicitly in the deliverables of the previous phases. In this way, you sequence your phases as a learning curriculum.

In a learning curriculum, there are prerequisite courses. Prerequisite courses need to be frontloaded. Your prerequisite courses are knowledge blocks without which your initiative cannot work. For example: the knowledge that the technology works; the knowledge that the market needs this product; the knowledge that our legacy computer systems can be connected. Delivering these knowledge blocks obviously needs to be frontloaded in your execution sequence. If the technology didn't work, or if your legacy computer systems couldn't be connected, whatever else is in your execution sequence really doesn't matter.

For an example of how a company we worked with identified its learning agenda, refer to 'Selling the derivatives'.

Selling the derivatives

A team from a European petrochemicals company was investigating how to improve the profitability of their petrochemical plants. In the past, the company had simply sold by-products from the plant directly in the market, typically at whatever profit margin they could realize. Now the company planned to gain additional value from selected by-products, by upgrading and selling the derivatives at an advantageous price.

As part of scoping its initiative, the team established a list of learning prerequisites:

♦ **There is a market for these derivative products.** Which customers from which industries will buy these products?

♦ **Customers will be willing to change to a new supplier.** Why will they buy our products?

♦ **We can leverage our existing business model.** Can we market, sell and deliver these products with our existing infrastructure? Will we need to team up with a partner company to do this?

♦ **We can sell these products profitably.** How much could we reasonably expect to sell and in what price range? What would be our cost of sales? How profitable will the venture be?

♦ **This business will remain profitable.** How cyclical are prices in these markets? Who are the major competitors? What are the barriers to new entrants?

Frontload the net cash flows

When you look at the net present value analysis of your future cash flows, this recommendation seems obvious. Yet, many execution plans ignore it. Practically, it means: sequence your execution phases so that your initiative starts contributing to the bottom line as early as possible. What is in your pocket is in your pocket. What is just promised is not in your pocket and may never get there.

Many initiatives keep delivering promises, milestone after milestone, until the very end, just to find out at that point that the money is not there. It goes like this: 'We have completed this task right on time!' – 'Great, and does it make money?' – 'Just wait until you see it!' Next phase: 'We are absolutely on budget, cost-wise and investment-wise!' – 'Great, and does it make money?' – 'Just wait until you see it!' Everything is delivered as promised, according to plan. All reports to top management enthusiastically refer to this brilliant execution. But there is no proof of the pudding yet. And the longer the time-frame to deliver real money, the lower the probability that it will ever happen.

When you frontload critical learning and cash flows, what you are saying is: 'It works and it makes money!' You need to sequence your execution phases, to the extent possible, in such a way that you can say this as early and as often as possible. This means that you need to design your phases with small increments and rapid market feedback. Fast prototyping to get fast feedback. 'Make mistakes early to learn faster', as recommended by David Kelley, the founder and CEO of IDEO.

Don't make commitments that don't have to be made

The feedback you get through this process can be somewhat more refined than 'Yes, it works' or 'No, it doesn't work'. It is often: 'Yes, it works under these and those conditions.' Or 'Yes, the product would gain market accept-ance if we could offer this feature.' In those cases, your subsequent phases begin to look like real options, and they need to be designed and sequenced like real options, with 'if – then' branches in your execution roadmap.

We will refer to this learning-dependent sequencing of execution phases as *agile* execution. *Agile* execution is like sailing: the sailing plan to get to your destination evolves to include real-time information on the wind, the tide, the latest weather forecast, and so on.

For example, try just a few features of this great new process with a limited sample of users. This can be done relatively quickly. Listen to the feedback, add some features, and try again. The feedback says: 'It works here, but maybe this is because of that condition that doesn't exist elsewhere.' So, try it again in a bigger pilot and learn from the feedback.

Working for many months on the perfect process without ever getting real feedback on real deliverables is sure to deliver an irrelevant output. We have seen initiatives deliver, after years of hard work, products that the market did not need any longer.

So, keep your options open for as long as you can. Preserve the possibility, at the end of each phase, at each deliverable, to reroute your execution according to what you have learned, according to context changes, according to the new opportunities that have materialized.

Get feedback on your roadmap

Before moving on with detailed planning and execution, you need again to get feedback from the future users of the initiative outcome. As we have seen, they will be solicited frequently during the execution to provide feedback on pilots. Their perspective on sequencing execution is obviously useful, and critical because you will need their continued support.

Clearly, you also need feedback from your providers of resources. The timing of their probable intervention depends on the sequencing of phases. But they also need to understand the contingent nature of your roadmap. Depending on which options you call as your execution progresses, the nature and timing of their intervention could change. You want their cooperation in this journey right from the start.

Last, but not least, you again want your roadmap to be challenged by your sponsor – but, certainly, this has already happened a few times! You have had your nose to the grindstone all along. In the sequencing work that you have just completed, it is very easy to lose sight of the destination. There are lots of possible routes to be compared. You need your sponsor to remind you of the execution priorities and to help you see which routes don't even need your attention.

Sponsor, another special piece of advice: this is also a time when it is vital that you explore with the team all the 'What if...?' questions. There are many that need to be explored in this *agile* roadmapping. Your help is critical here, and it's a time to get your hands dirty working with the team. Remember: the output of this effort is the route chart to execute your strategic initiative. It will give you and the team the necessary perspective when it's time to call options. These will be big decisions, and we will discuss them later. From now on, it's execution and you will need that route map.

Chart your course

Scoping your initiative can be compared to marking your route options on a chart before a long-haul sea trip. It doesn't get into every detail. Its purpose is to identify and examine your main sailing options. Later, it will serve as a reference for key decisions. Scoping is a team task. It helps the team transform an assigned initiative into *their* journey. It involves several discussions with the sponsor to challenge the thinking of the team, compare options and finally agree on a common scope.

According to one source on the history of cartography, it was the Egyptians who pioneered map-making. As the Nile flooded their land annually, they needed maps to help locate where to expect water in the future so they could avoid putting buildings or crops in that endangered location. Experts even have an Egyptian map that dates back to 1300 BC.[4] That's a long time ago, we realize, yet – in its own way – this is a form of crude but important execution scoping.

You and your business may not be worried about water encroaching on your crops, but there are many details tied to any strategic initiative that need to be mapped *before* you begin the execution stage. If you and your execution team don't set your course, who will?

---

4 'The history of cartography'
(http://www-groups.dcs.st-and.ac.uk/~history/HistTopics/Cartography.html.

Play to win

IN OUR INTRODUCTION to this book, we noted that the seven insights we want to share with you are equally important. We say that because we have seen instances where managers did *most* things right, but failed to note the importance of one or more of the seven insights. As a result, their inattention created a barrier and their strategic initiative was far from successful (if it survived at all).

The American Management Association (AMA) commissioned the Human Resource Institute to survey more than 1,500 managers worldwide early in 2007. The subject? Strategy execution. On the plus side, the survey supported what we have long believed: 'Organizations that were good at executing strategies were also more likely to cite success in the marketplace, as measured by self-reported revenue growth, market share, profitability, and customer satisfaction.' This, of course, is the reason we are so motivated to help you and others execute strategy far better than it's being done.

So much for the good news. What of the bad? The survey results speak for themselves:

- Only three per cent of the executives said that their companies executed their strategy successfully.
- Sixty-two per cent of the executives thought their companies were executing their strategy in a moderately successful (or worse!) way.

AMA's president, Edward T. Reilly, studied the complete survey results and concluded, 'The findings show that strategy execution can improve as executives learn how to focus and align daily activities to strategic goals. To ensure this, top leaders must be committed to clear, direct, and constant communication, and committed to the change necessary to implement evolving strategies.'[1]

Committed to win

Top-level sports champions and their coaches know that superb technical expertise is a requirement but is not in itself enough to achieve success. To be successful, athletes also require what is referred to as 'mental energy' – a huge motivation to win.

There are similarities between high-level sports competition and strategic initiatives. They are not 'more of the same'. They require novel approaches and new efforts in many parts of the organization. They require a high level of coordination. They require sustained energy. They require mental concentration to provide well-thought-out responses to changing environments. They require the same determination to win that top-level sports champions have. They are not for amateurs.

Execution logic is rarely the main problem with strategic initiatives. Most of the time the logic is clear enough – and yet nothing happens. But how often do we hear 'yes, but' from the execution side? 'Yes, it seems a good idea, but I am not sure it's for me.' People nod, but they are still on the other side of the fence. Commitment is not there: it's a situation that is set up to fail. Strategic initiatives leave no room for 'yes, but' faltering.

Allow us now to ask you an intriguing question: *where does the energy to win come from?*

We hear you answer: 'From the guts!' Bizarrely, common wisdom is that knowledge workers have energy from their guts, while athletes have mental energy. What common wisdom probably means is that energy comes from the whole body. Energy comes from a physical state of well-being. It comes from optimal physiological coordination. This physical state gives you a sense of power and freedom to act. You feel the capacity to master how you interact with your social environment, whether it is in the family, at work, with friends or with strangers.

---

[1] See AMA Press Release of 19 March 2007 (http://press.amanet.org/press-releases/97/most-companies-are-only-moderately-successful – or-worse – when-it-comes-to-executing-strategy-executives-say/).

This sense of physical and physiological well-being is an emotional state. An emotional state manifests itself through temporary physical and physiological body reactions. Examples are increased heartbeat, muscular tension, shivers. These temporary body changes are reflected in our consciousness as feelings. You are conscious of your energy because you feel good, strong, optimistic. Overall, being conscious of your energy gives you pleasure. And when you feel blue, you have no energy; that gives you pain.

You feel energetic and happy when you are in certain modes of social interaction at work, with people you know well or with strangers. You feel depressed and unhappy when you are in certain other modes of social interaction. Those that you prefer to be in are marked with positive emotions. So you feel energized, and they give you pleasure. Conversely, the modes of social interaction that you would rather avoid depress you when you get caught in them. They are marked with negative emotions. You feel it in your stomach. They are just painful.

We suggest that you say 'yes, but' when you are not yet sure whether the mode of social interaction you are being pushed into will give you pleasure or pain. Of course, when you have the choice, you seek the mode of social interaction that gives you most pleasure. This is where you feel at your best. It has worked for you in the past. You had impact on your context. And the more you have this positive experience, the stronger its emotional marker and the more you seek it.

Thus, we believe (at those times when you are *sure* that you can achieve success in a life or business strategy) that your energy can come from several different motivational sources. Let's review the key ones.

Social motives

A person's preferred mode of social interaction is often referred to as that person's *main social motive.* You are motivated to put your energy in this particular form of social interaction because you find it rewarding. 'Motivation is not an emotion per se,' observes John Ratey, a professor of psychiatry at Harvard University, 'but a process that ties emotion to action. Motivation is the director of emotions. It determines how much energy and attention the brain and the body assign to a given stimulus'[2] (for example, to a given social context).

---

[2] John Ratey, *A User's Guide to the Brain*, Abacus, 2001, pp.247 and 310.

It has been suggested that there are three preferred modes of social interaction, or *social motives*, that human beings have. Different people prefer one or the other. In other words, because of your genetic legacy, because of your education, because of your life experience, one or the other of these social motives is more strongly marked emotionally for you as giving you energy and pleasure.

- *Achievement-recognition*: people with this social motive seek recognition from their social context for high achievements.
- *Power*: people with this social motive seek to take control of their social context.
- *Affiliation*: people with this social motive seek to befriend with their social context.

Some people are dominated by one of these social motives, while others combine them.

Aiming high

Ken, a leader whose mobilization effectiveness we have been able to observe many times, had a maxim: 'ambitious and achievable targets'. This principle challenges *high achievers* to be not only ambitious but also to push the limits of what is achievable. You will certainly recognize that it applies to your strategic initiative. 'More of the same' would clearly not work for you.

Psychologists describe *high achievers* as motivated by setting targets that they want to beat.[3] Often, however, this doesn't necessarily mean the highest possible targets. High achievers want their targets to be high enough to constitute an achievement, but not so high that they present a serious execution risk. Indeed, the ultimate purpose of high achievers is to get *recognition*, not only in their own eyes but also in the eyes of others. They maintain a tight balance between aiming high enough to get recognition, and not aiming so high that they might miss the recognition. The challenge is to get them to push the limits of ambition and achievability, without losing the motivation effect.

To discuss how to get the best out of high achievers, let's look at one of your team members, Liu, a classic high achiever. Liu responds quite

---

[3] See in particular *Human Motivation*, David C. McClelland, Cambridge University Press, 1987, pp. 223–67.

positively to the challenge of pushing the limits. In fact, he would be disappointed if you did not challenge him for more demanding targets. Pushing the limits, however, needs to be done skilfully. If you push too far, the risk of failure increases, and Liu begins to fear that he will not get recognition for his achievement.

An ambitious target is a record to beat, and Liu is competitive. The opportunity to surpass his previous performance, or someone else's performance, will stimulate his motivation. You may want to insist on the mission-critical character of a task. Or you may point out that some people believe that it cannot be done. Or you may want to emphasize that there is an opportunity to do something unique. Liu likes to go for innovative approaches. These incentives will increase his motivation.

In order to deserve personal recognition, Liu also needs to have ownership of his targets. Top–down directives and micromanagement will demotivate Liu because of the fear that he will not get recognition for his actions. His targets must emerge from an open discussion and a real debate. In the end, Liu will refer to his goals as personal commitments, much more than as commitments to you. But when to stop pushing obviously needs attention from you as a sponsor or team leader.

At the same time as pushing for ambitious targets, it is also important to verify that they are achievable to retain their motivational impact on Liu. Reviewing in detail how they will be achieved will help. Possible pathways should be compared, supporting facts analysed, and assumptions checked. You need to go through these steps with Liu to confirm with him the achievability of his ambitious goals – without which recognition could be missed.

Of course, performance feedback and recognition are absolutely critical for Liu. Actually, Liu takes full responsibility for his results. He never looks for excuses nor does he ever blame the rest of the world for what happens to him. So, investigative control and no follow-up at all are effective ways to kill his motivation. For him, follow-up is to discuss with you what he will do next. And, even though Liu may come across as quite autonomous and entrepreneurial, explicit recognition is needed.

Obviously, you want people like Liu in your team. Their energy is easy to turn on. They are motivated by pushing the limits of ambition and achievability. But their energy is also easy to turn off. Not enough, too much, or no recognition can easily do that. Pushing the limits of ambition and achievability is hard work for Liu and for yourself. An absent-landlord sponsor will be neither effective nor credible doing it.

Power players

For your initiative to progress at the necessary pace, you want people who take things into their own hands. As we have said, surges of energy are frequently needed. Strategic initiatives compete with other organizational activities. Deadlines are tight. Temptations to let go, to say 'this is good enough', are frequent.

So, you want in your team people who, relentlessly, want to get things done. Interestingly, according to psychologists, these people are motivated by a high need for power.[4] Perhaps this leaves you perplexed. How many people with a high need for power do you really want in your team?

People with a high *power motive*, in fact, are of two kinds. Some have a high need for *personal power* and simply like power for its own sake. Some have a high need for *institutional influence* and put their motive at the service of the organization.[5] This sounds better, doesn't it?

People with a high *personal power* motive are indeed a problem. Their ego is generally voluminous. They think in terms of power struggles and win–lose. They are centralizers. They exercise their power by controlling access to resources, to information and to other people. They enjoy prestige symbols. Some are obsessed with having the love and admiration of others and can easily be narcissistic. When, in addition, they are *the* specialist of a particular capability that you badly need, this is a recipe for disaster. People with a need for high personal power demotivate others. They should simply be avoided in your team.

People with a high need for *institutional influence* also have a power motive. But it is mitigated by their social–emotional maturity. They are able to control their drive to dominate others and to apply it to socially accept-able outlets, such as putting it at the service of the organization. They like to influence others, they are emotionally and socially self-reliant, and they are hard workers. These people need managing, but, potentially, they bring with them a lot of execution energy. They can also be effective leaders.[6]

To discuss how to get the best out of people with a high need for *institutional power*, let's now turn to another of your team members, Maggie. As an *institutional-power* person, Maggie is a classic.

---

[4] David C. McClelland, ibid, pp. 268–332.
[5] David C. McClelland, ibid, p. 282.
[6] *Power is the Great Motivator*, David McClelland and David Burnham, Harvard Business Review, vol. 54, 1976.

First of all, Maggie just enjoys action. Involvement, getting things done, being hands-on will give her the sense of being in control. For example, you will notice an increase in her motivation when moving from planning to execution. Maggie will also be more willing than the high achievers to take risks. But, sometimes, her urge for action can also result in activism.

She is a very hard worker, even a workaholic. She works hard because it is her way to control things in a socially acceptable way. So she is also a valuable source of energy for your team. You must be careful not to discourage her, for example, when she is keen to do more and to take initiatives.

Maggie can give the impression of sacrificing herself for the strategic initiative. She may not think that she is, because she has set her own pressure cooker. But she is: her life balance can suffer. She may also drive others hard. As sponsor or team leader you need to watch and to help her avoid personal disasters.

Because of her low reliance on others, Maggie may also be a loner. Her hard work, abnegation and strong self-control can be intimidating to others. This may complicate matters within your team. But she could also find an outlet in coaching others. It can be a win–win situation. But perhaps you may want to give her some training in coaching so that the initiative does not turn into a boot camp.

Of course, being given responsibility for a piece of the action will greatly motivate Maggie. She seems capable and the situation can again be a win–win. Some sponsors or team leaders, however, may not see the opportunity because they want to retain control for themselves. Having the potential to be a good leader, having responsibility for parts of the execution with some autonomy, will be developmental and motivating for Maggie.

It is not difficult to imagine that someone like Maggie is also likely to be fairly assertive. Her need to influence the thinking of others through arguments comes with the profile. It may sometimes be annoying, but it is not bad. Disagreement is helpful in a strategic-initiative team. This propensity to question and challenge is in fact an indispensable resource. You want people who challenge the thinking, who look at issues from a different perspective and who question the status quo. But you would prefer her to argue without the urge to win the argument. For example, you want her to learn how to present her arguments as questions, encouraging feedback, rather than as definitive conclusions.[7]

---

[7] The 'advocacy-inquiry' approach was proposed by Chris Argyris and Donald A. Schön, in several books and articles, but in particular in *Organizational Learning: Theory, Method and Practice*, Addison Wesley, 1995.

Of course, you also want some team members like Maggie in your strategic-initiative team. They are not easy to manage, but they contribute a lot of energy. They need coaching to learn how to control their propensity to dominate while getting the best out of it. But, on the other hand, their energy is readily available. They are self-starters. Looking at it from a developmental point of view, strategic initiatives are also a great opportunity for them to build on their potential and to expand their leadership capabilities.

Team dynamic

The ability of your team to work effectively as a team is also a source of energy to execute your strategic initiative. You need your team to be more than the sum of its members.

Strategic-initiative teams are typically formed from specialists who are only familiar with one piece of the action, but who need to deliver an integrated solution together. So, they depend on each other for delivering. They need to learn fast how to get the best out of their mutual dependency. They are jointly accountable for delivering on all dimensions of the strategic initiative, so they also need to learn fast how to handle that. When people refer to the need for *integrative* capabilities in a team, this is what they mean: the capabilities to work with mutual dependency and joint accountability.

There was nothing in Liu's motives that prevented him from being an effective team member. But there was nothing either that would give him an urge to put his energy into integrative teamwork. He would probably walk away from it if he found that he would achieve more on his own. Maggie quite probably likes the idea of having a team to run. Whether the team works in an integrative way or not is probably not her major concern. So you also want in your team people who have the drive to integrate talented players into a winning team.

Could someone with a high need for *affiliation* do that? There are two kinds of people with a high affiliation motive.[8] Some like to work in teams because it just feels nice to be with others, while some use their integrative capabilities to make their team more productive. To some extent they are not mutually exclusive, but the former alone is far from sufficient for your strategic initiative.

---

[8] David C. McClelland, pp. 333–72.

The people who see a team essentially as a social occasion come with a few characteristics that are not very helpful in getting execution energy.[9]

- They need to form relationships with others because they depend on them for their own reassurance. This motive is self-serving, and they are often perceived as using others for their own emotional comfort.

- Nevertheless, they see their social contribution as valuable – and seek confirmation that it is. They will find themselves a role in 'touchy-feely' undertakings, such as navel-gazing and soul-searching. They will be frustrated at the suggestion that it might be time to move on.

- In a task, they value the interpersonal aspects, but they are not particularly preoccupied with delivering results. They value socializing and enjoy informal activities.

- They do their best to avoid conflicts (in some organizations, this is a valued contribution). Avoiding rejection is one of their strongest motives. They like to agree and they are the kind of people you can turn to in a discussion: they will always nod at you approvingly.

According to research, these people generally do not perform well as managers. They are not able to confront difficult tasks and interpersonal issues because they fear disrupting relationships.[10] To be honest, some of their motives are helpful. Their desire for harmonious interpersonal relations helps diverse people to become socially acquainted so as to be able to work together. There are times when teams need such skills.

Two things are missing, however. First, self-interest doesn't really work to build harmonious interpersonal relations. The whole team must be better off, not just the cheerleader. Second, harmonious interpersonal relationships for the sake of them alone is not good enough. You want them to be productive also because there is an initiative to execute.

Let's look at another member of your team, Tessie, a classic *team integrator*. First of all, she has some of the motives that the high-affiliation people have. She is at ease with people, but not only with people who agree with her. She likes the company of people with whom she can have good arguments. Tessie doesn't mind conflicts. Her view is that there is always something productive coming out of them. She is a mountain climber and

---

[9] David C. McClelland, ibid, pp. 348–59.

[10] John J. Gabarro, *A Brief Note on Social Motives*, Harvard Business School (9-477-053), 1980.

she can tell you about the arguments they have when they plan their next ascent – until they are roped together; then it's a different story.

Tessie also knows a lot of people. She is extremely resourceful when it comes to knowing someone who could help with a particular task. And it always sounds as if that 'someone' was just waiting for her call. As a result, she is also an invaluable go-between. She likes to connect people who she knows will benefit.

Now, Tessie has two more motives that are very important for the energy of your team:

◆ The first is that she is driven by the belief that a team can achieve results that no individual alone can. This sounds like a fairly obvious notion, but many people, particularly those like Liu and Maggie, give up on this idea because of the complication of working as a team.

◆ The second is that she will never hesitate to support team members who need help. They may need resources or moral support; she will be their Mother Teresa.

Let us start with her second motive. Mutual support in a team is not just a matter of being nice to each other. Mutual support is necessary because of the mutual dependency of the members of a strategic-initiative team. Teams are not made stronger by having the best people do more – Liu and Maggie might try that. What makes them effective is when those experiencing difficulties get support to perform better. This mutual support is required in the shape of ideas and suggestions, sharing information, sharing resources, learning from each other, as well as moral support when one feels blue.

Mobilizing mutual support is Tessie's strength as a team integrator. She keeps reminding her teammates that, if anyone is left lagging, the whole team will suffer. 'It is really rewarding when a manager is concerned about the team as a whole reaching the deadlines and is willing to lend someone a hand to catch up,' noted one executive.

Thanks to Tessie, team members also learn that they should ask for help when they need it. They realize that, if they don't ask for help, everyone else in the team will suffer. Not asking for help is letting the team down, not the other way around. Perhaps this notion will be somewhat counter-intuitive for Liu and Maggie.

People like Tessie are genuinely interested in their fellow human beings. In your initiative team, you see them pay attention to every team member and care for their needs. Psychologists refer to this motive as the *intimacy motive*.[11] But don't get scared. People with intimacy motives value warmth, sincerity, appreciation of others and attention to others – nothing dangerous. But in many organizations, individualism prevails and these motives are discouraged, if not scorned.

As we have seen, in a strategic-initiative team, the counterpart of mutual dependency is joint accountability. Being jointly under pressure for results, team members need to mind each other's business. They must all feel responsible for any aspect of the initiative and start probing each other. As a result, they will understand each other's perspectives better and become more willing to give in instead of pushing their own views. Progressively the team will converge towards a robust common perspective.

In many organizations, this is just not done. You simply mind your own business. But in your team, integrators like Tessie will make sure that this is not the case. She will create opportunities for Maggie to start asking questions and probing. And perhaps there is a dose of Maggie's motives in Tessie. Liu will actually seize the opportunity to see whether the limits couldn't be pushed further. Perhaps there is also a dose of Liu's motives in Tessie.

Now, Tessie's ability to handle tensions and conflicts will be very helpful. She is good at opening the cupboards so that the skeletons can come out. She is good at steering peer pressure in a positive way. Tessie's speciality is *supportive challenge*: challenging each other for results in a supportive way. Without it, a strategic-initiative team of people like Liu and Maggie could never perform in an integrated manner.

Almost ready

Now you have in your team a mix of people like Liu, Maggie and Tessie. Together, they bring the motives that are needed to make the execution successful. This is as much potential energy as you will ever get. Shouldn't action follow automatically, then?

Well, you are presenting to them the proposed initiative, how critical it is as a strategic priority, how it will change the future of the company. And they are staring at you, still on the other side of the fence. They ask a few questions to confirm the logic of the argument. You have the answers, the logic is perfect and they admit it. And you see them still on the other side of the fence. You brag about the quality of the team that you have been able to

---

[11] David C. McClelland, 1987, p. 360.

assemble. You suggest that being on the team will give them visibility and will advance their careers. You hint that top management is watching. This brings a few smiles to their faces. But they are still on the other side of the fence. What is missing?

Commitment from them?

What is missing is their decision to commit to applying their motives to the initiative you are presenting. This is a new situation for all of them. How do they decide to commit their energy to it? Where does commitment come from? Why is it still missing? Shouldn't action immediately follow motivation?

The expression 'emotional commitment' is often used – rather imprecisely – to refer to any motivation that is difficult to explain with strict logic. What has emotion to do with this? If it is logical, commitment will necessarily follow, many people believe. In fact, haven't we learned that sound decision-making keeps emotions out? Show once more the logic of the argument and the smart guys will see the point. This is the thinking that has made the fortune of PowerPoint®.

Yet, many people sense that emotion might have a place in all this. Hasn't emotion been somewhat rehabilitated by management gurus? 'Having fun', for example, is supposed to help. Shouldn't good leaders know how to dose emotion to 'energize' their troops? A dose at the beginning, like pulling the choke. A few doses at scheduled meetings, to 'recharge the batteries'. And a last dose when it's all over, to 'celebrate'. For sure, these leaders know where the plug in the wall is and they are not the kind who leave their charger at home.

Well, here is some news. Without emotion and feelings, you cannot make decisions about your own future in relation to your social context – any decision that allows you to manage your future well-being. Without emotion and feelings, you cannot turn your motives into action. So, you cannot make up your mind to commit, and to sustain your commitment, to the execution of a new strategic initiative.

This is not really a new idea. It goes back to Plato, Aristotle, Spinoza, William James, just for name dropping. But neuroscience, and the technical possibility to monitor neural activity fairly accurately, has more than confirmed the fact. Neuroscientists may still not completely agree on how it works in detail, but none of them would disagree with the view that emotions are indispensable to decision-making. There is substantial evidence that patients with lesions in brain areas where emotions are processed are unable to decide on their future well-being. Most could work out that the net present value of a project is higher than the cost of capital, if they had been told how to do it. But they could not make the decision to invest their own money.

Commitment from you?

We propose that you move across the fence and now look at your exhortation to the team from their perspective.

This is a high-level description of how you decide to commit. We will start from a situation that requires that you make the decision whether to join a strategic-initiative team and to put your energy to it. We will end with your decision either to commit wholeheartedly with full energy, to wait and see, to go through the motions reluctantly without energy or to flee, find an excuse and escape the dilemma.

The situation: the strategic-initiative presentation

You have been asked to join the team entrusted with the execution of this critical strategic initiative. The sponsor of the initiative is presenting it at a management meeting. The initiative itself seems quite logical. It's time for you to make up your mind.

It's a serious commitment with heavy implications. There are uncertainties about how things might unfold, particularly for you. There are time conflicts with your other tasks. You don't know how it will be to work with that sponsor and that team. You are thinking of your family with whom you already do not spend enough time. There are clear pains in the short term; will there be enough rewards in the long term?

As much as your sponsor would like his slides to trigger immediate support, there is no automatic response coming to your mind.

Emotional signals

On paper, this is an impossible decision. You just can't draw that decision tree. There are too many pieces of information, leading to too many options, leading to too many uncertain outcomes.

The conductor of your brain, your frontal lobes,[12] looks for patterns in that chaos. A pattern is a set of facts that has been experienced before, with

---

[12] 'The frontal lobes are to the brain what a conductor is to an orchestra, a general to an army, the chief executive officer to a corporation.' Elkhonon Goldberg, *The Executive Brain: Frontal Lobes and the Civilized Mind*, Oxford University Press, 2001, p. 2.

the options that were selected and their good or bad outcomes. Throughout evolution, creatures seeking to master their future, like us, have learned to mark these patterns as they repeat with an emotional state and the resulting feelings. This is as if they had been painted with a colour code: red for danger, green for satisfaction. They are marked with a feeling of happiness or pain. From a perspective of maintaining our future well-being, this is a very effective and efficient reference-library system. Antonio Damasio, a neuroscientist who is one of the pioneers in studying the role of emotion in complex personal decisions, first proposed this hypothesis in the 1990s and it is now well accepted.[13]

So, while listening to the strategic-initiative presentation, whenever your brain conductor spots a pattern, the emotional signal associated with it is being revived. This emotional signal produces an overt or covert temporary change in your body state. More importantly, the outcome associated with this pattern is revealed to you by a more or less conscious feeling, like happiness or fear.

For example, Maggie's brain conductor spots an opportunity to be in control and to run things. Maggie feels good. This is how the conductor tells Maggie, 'Go for it'. Now, Maggie can't wait to get started. This initiative will be her chance to make a difference.

Or Liu's brain conductor spots a pattern of heavy top–down control. He feels uneasy. If the signal is strong enough he may sigh, cough, swallow. This is how his conductor tells him, 'Watch out!' Liu is already looking for ways to escape this trap.

Narrowing the options

'The revival of the emotional signal accomplishes a number of important tasks,' observes Antonio Damasio. He continues: 'Covertly or overtly, it focuses attention on certain aspects of the problem and thus enhances the quality of reasoning over it.'[14]

So, first, the recalled emotional signal narrows the attention of our brain conductor to those options that matter. They matter either because, when they were selected, a positive outcome ensued or because of the contrary.

[13] Antonio Damasio, *Descartes' Error: Emotion, Reason, and the Human Brain*, New York, 1994.
[14] Antonio Damasio, *Looking For Spinoza: Joy, Sorrow, and the Feeling Brain*, Harcourt, 2003, p. 147.

Second, the recalled emotional signal increases the probability that the options that yielded positive outcomes in prior experiences will be reused – or that the options that yielded bad outcomes will be avoided.

Sometimes, the emotional signal is quite strong. You really sense it in your body just like the last time you experienced this pattern. You smile from ear to ear. You nod enthusiastically. You feel genuinely happy, optimistic and energized. Or, if the news is bad, you really feel tense, depressed, sad. You just follow your gut feeling, believing that you have made a decision.

In most instances, however, you feel neither happy nor particularly sad. In other words, you do not sense a strong body confirmation, accompanied with explicit feelings. It doesn't mean that the body and the feelings are not involved, but it is 'nothing to write home about'. You just have a hunch. 'The hunches that steer our behavior in the proper direction are often referred to as the gut or the heart – as in "I know in my heart that this is the right thing to do",' explains Antonio Damasio. Portuguese being his mother tongue, he adds, 'The Portuguese word for *hunch*, by the way, is *palpite*, a close neighbor of "palpitation", a skipped heartbeat.'[15]

Do you proceed?

You believe that you have made the right decision. You have not decided, in the sense of applying explicit reasoning strategies. It was all suggested to you by your emotions. But without emotion you would not have been able to decide anything anyway. 'Contrary to the popular notion that decision making requires a cool head, it is feelings that point us in the right direction and help us make moral, personal, predictive, and planning decisions,' observes John Ratey.[16] Antonio Damasio's team has conducted research suggesting that your brain knows what the right strategy is before you become conscious of what that strategy is.[17]

[15] Antonio Damasio, ibid, p. 150.
[16] John Ratey, *A User's Guide to the Brain*, p. 310.
[17] Antoine Bechara, Hanna Damasio, Daniel Tranel, Antonio R. Damasio, 'Deciding Advantageously Before Knowing the Advantageous Decision', *Science*, 28 February 1997, vol. 275, p. 1293.

'Reasonable' choice

Contrary to orthodox managerial persuasion, your hunches are not to be dismissed. Your brain conductor has followed a very rational, fact-based path. It is eminently 'reasonable'.[18] In most instances, you will be able to reason out and verbalize your choice explicitly.

You could even rethink the whole thing and decide to act against your hunch. Most of the time, actually, when you do this, it is because you don't have a choice. We certainly do things that are not in our best apparent long-term interest to avoid an even worse immediate outcome. An example is losing one's job. If that were the outcome, all the rest becomes irrelevant.

So, even though you might get a very strong hunch that this strategic initiative is going to be misery for you, your explicit reasoning will conclude that you should still go through the motions. Otherwise, your career might be stopped, your mentor might be disappointed and drop you, you could lose face in front of your peers, or worse. To avoid these disasters, you accept a miserable life. Negative emotions will plague you. Your physiological equilibria will deteriorate. Some people go through a burn-out. Some people become seriously ill. Or, to take revenge on their torturers and their allies, some people become cynics. Either way, it's a lose–lose. You probably don't want this to happen in your team.

Who knows how you made up your mind?

What led you to commit to the strategic initiative – or, indeed, not to commit – is far from transparent even to yourself. So, how could anyone else ever hope to 'motivate' you to join the initiative and apply your energy to it? In fact, if anything, it seems a lot easier for any leader to demotivate you than to motivate you.

Committing to the uncertain future offered by a strategic initiative is a very complex decision. There are dozens of questions to ask, such as:

Who knows what's in your library of prior experiences? Who knows how strong the emotional markers are that you have attached to these experiences over the years? (Not even you.) *Who knows which features of the current strategic initiative have awakened prior experiences and recalled emotional states and feelings?* (Not even you.) *Who knows which social motives have*

---

[18] Stephan P. Heck, *Reasonable Behavior: Making the Public Sensible*, University of California, San Diego, 1998. Quoted by A. Damasio, op.cit., p. 150.

guided your emotional response to the initiative and, eventually, your hunch? (With some introspection, you could probably find out. But your sponsor and the other team members may not know you yet.) *Who knows what your hunch is on this issue?* (You probably know, but who else does?)

So, what do you think your leader can do to get you on the other side of the fence? As we are going to see, very little in terms of direct intervention, but quite a lot indirectly, shaping the context of your commitment.

What can the leader do?

After reflecting on how you decide to commit to an initiative, let's get back to the other side of the fence. As a leader, what can you do to facilitate the commitment of those you want to get on your side of the fence?

Let's look first at what you cannot do. In many companies, for example, the previous experiences with strategic initiatives have not been great. How many times are you ready to repeat that, this time, it will be different? In fact, your team members will also have lots of other memories, on authority, on trust, on rewards or lack thereof. None of it can be changed. You need to prove that the context has changed, and the proof of the pudding is in the eating.

Some companies propose to communicate more and better why the initiative is critical. One company we worked with suggested training their line managers to communicate the importance of the iniative more effectively to their hesitating troops. But, as we have seen, it is not the lack of logic that is most likely to get in the way of commitment.

We have also seen companies suggest that the solution is in better discipline. This is just another way of saying, 'Please, be committed!' And it will just achieve the same effects. It is commitment that gets shared discipline, not authority-based discipline that gets commitment. So, go back to square one: go for commitment first.

Yet, more communication and more discipline are the two main remedies that many companies cling to when they try to stimulate commitment to their strategic initiatives. Instead, to stimulate commitment, to instil a winning spirit, we suggest that you start from the perspective that executing a strategic initiative is an emotional experience. As we have seen, this doesn't mean a touchy-feely experience. It should no longer make you uncomfortable. There are many hard facts to address to get there. And, in that emotional experience, you are the conductor: you set the pace; then, you get the best out of your talented musicians.

First, look at yourself

To better understand how a sports coach would address the challenge of inspiring energy to a player, we asked a golf champion: 'Anna,[19] how would you work with a player who has had miserable results for the last few months, and is now just about to play in a very important tournament?' Anna's response was immediate: 'First, look at yourself!' Anna continued: 'If you are not feeling full of energy yourself for the project, just forget it. If you are not convinced that this player can win, don't even try! Then, pick even a moderate success that this player has had, and blow it out of proportion!'

The point is, if you want to energize others, start with yourself. If you want to instil commitment, start with yourself. We have seen too many strategic initiatives in which the sponsor, for example, was standing aloof on the side of the track, cheering occasionally, but not really present. It could have been any team on any initiative. Even jumping up and down while painting the great future will not do it. In the same way as a faked smile (cheeeeese...) will not fool anyone, faked energy will not work.

As a leader, you may only increase lukewarm energy and commitment through contagion. In fact, it is emotions that are often contagious. How do babies learn to smile? Why do people cry at the funeral of a person they hardly know? Why does a smiling person cheer you up? Neuroscientists have precisely identified in primates neurons that fire when observing an action and when performing the same action. They have designated them as 'mirror neurons'. Mirror neurons are believed to exist in human brains also, since the same phenomenon can be observed with humans. An apprentice fires neural connections in the same brain areas when observing her master and when doing the job herself (actually, a stronger response is observed with women than with men).

These mirror-neuron areas support social functions that are important to you as a leader. One is the detection and understanding of the intentions of another person. Leaders are more transparent than they believe. For example, faking energy and commitment to enrol team members for a new initiative is easily detected. This is the reason why, instead, rationality is so often overemphasized – and overdone. But, if your intentions are what you

---

[19] Anna Dunand-Lindblom, a colleague of ours, was a member of the Swedish National Golf Team for eight years. She also played for several years in the USA. She trained with some of the best coaches in the world and she has been a coach herself.

say they are, the gut feelings in your team will be: 'She is genuine, she really means it! I can trust her.'

Another function is empathy, or emotion appreciation. Through empathy you become aware of the motives of another person and you are able to respond. Women are generally recognized as doing this better than men. On the receiving end, people sense that their motives are supported. The gut feelings in your team will be: 'This will work, I will have a chance to do my best and she wants me to do so!'

So, first, look at yourself, because the others are watching you, with more insight than we might normally imagine, to decide on their conduct. This is in fact what is generally referred to as 'walking the talk'. It also has to do with the frequent advice to leaders to be 'authentic', or to be themselves, because this is all that will work. It is the only chance for the leader to challenge the dangerous memories that might be invoked at the beginning of the process and to say in a credible manner, 'I am trustworthy, come along.'

Second, get the best out of the people you work with

We asked Ken, whom we mentioned before: 'How do you get the best out of the people you work with?' Ken responded without hesitation: 'Personal interest in the persons who work with me!' And he added, 'Personal interest in their work, how they work, what help they need. But also personal interest in them as individuals, in their motives, in what gets them going.'

Ken had actually set up a process to make sure that he could manifest his empathy to his team members when they needed it: 'I get Human Resources to tell me if they, or someone in their family, are ill and then I go and ask how they are doing. Then, I follow up and ask again. This has a huge impact and puts smiles on the faces of people.'

Ken would stand next to you and grab your arm to give you feedback, as if he was talking with an old friend. We personally experienced his energizing empathy. He was always telling us how he enjoyed working with us and we learnt a great deal from him. We would never have let him down. So, just imagine how his team felt.

The interesting point is that Ken's attitude of empathy was emulated by his subordinates – as could be expected from the mirror-neurons theory – providing each of them with a secure emotional home base. The team members were under pressure from their leader to perform. But they gave each other strong mutual support. Contrary to popular belief, making emotions legitimate, as we saw, allows people to focus on the job in hand.

Your personal attention to individuals also allows you to understand and address their motives for committing to the strategic initiative. These motives, you will remember, 'are the director of emotion'. You discover them by observing which emotional reactions are linked to which behaviours. As we have just seen, it requires empathy, or, more generally, *interpersonal intelligence*, the ability to understand the emotions of others, and *intrapersonal intelligence*, the ability to use one's own emotions.[20]

Addressing the motives of people is often seen as anything between a 'nice-to-have' by-product, and a 'wishy-washy' waste of time. People should see that the initiative is important in itself and discipline should do the rest. As we have seen, logic has, at best, a very limited impact. And discipline is a risky way to get the job done. It arouses fear emotions as well as feelings of dependency, impotence and isolation. It focuses thinking on avoidance. On the contrary, the motives that we have discussed earlier, achievement-recognition, institutional influence and team integration, are worth addressing. They are a more likely way to get results. The rewards they are related to are recognition, influence, solidarity – something to go for.

You quite probably missed a curious bit of testimony from Mohan Murti, who was for a time the European director of the Confederation of Indian Industry. In an Internet posting in April 2007 on *BusinessLine*, Murti relates how he was in the Copenhagen airport lounge when he came across a friend of his from Germany. That friend was none other than Thomas Bach, who is a lawyer, someone with experience on the International Olympic Committee and the elected president of the German Olympic Sports Confederation.

Murti recounts how the talk between them quickly focused on sports – and, specifically, the excellence of European sports. Said Murti: 'The *raison d'être* of European triumph in sports, as I understood from Dr Thomas Bach, is careful talent identification, rigorous and painstakingly meticulous training and development, fair exposure to opportunities and a handsome rewards system.'[21] That's a nice summary of what we have been aiming to express throughout this chapter. No matter where you are in the execution of a strategic initiative, the time is *now* for you to set up to win.

---

[20] See, for example, Howard Gardner, *Frames of Mind*, Paladin Books, 1983, or *Multiple Intelligences*, 1993. These forms of intelligence have more recently been popularized as *emotional intelligence*. See, for example, *Emotional Intelligence*, Daniel Goleman, 1995, Bantam Books.
[21] 'Sport is more than a game in Europe', Mohan Murti, *BusinessLine*, 23 April, 2007 (http://www.blonnet.com/2007/04/23/stories/2007042300200900.htm).

5

Think it through

FERRARI ONLY SELLS about 4,000 sports cars per year. But at a price tag that can hit €180,000. To keep the quality high, the company actually *limits* the number of cars it can manufacture in any given period. It apparently wants each car to be of such style and class that the look and feel of Ferrari purrs forth, starting with the powerful vroom of the engine. We've wondered, from time to time, how it is that Ferrari can keep up – year after year – such a high standard. It was a premium car company when it first started producing high-powered cars for the masses in 1947. Now, 60 years later, it's still *avant garde*.

Mario Almondo, chief of human resources at Ferrari, addressed this subject in an issue of *Harvard Business Review*. Almondo reports how the company actually has a Creativity Club, open to all levels of its employees. The company stages small sessions with relatively few employees and then lets them engage with artists – painters, sculptors, writers, musicians, even chefs and other creative types – in the hope that the creative sparks will ultimately engender the level of style and class required for the marketplace of tomorrow.

'You can't methodically teach creativity,' says Almondo. 'But you can provide an environment that nurtures it... The goal is for our employees to learn about how artists generate ideas and solutions.'[1] Ponder, for a moment, the value-added (and, to our minds, the sheer genius) of such an exercise. The interaction of artists with Ferrari employees produces nothing

---

[1] 'Sparking Creativity at Ferrari', *Chair of Entrepreneurial Risks* (http://www.er.ethz.ch/news/ferrari).

at the moment – yet it can have enormous payoff down the line. The more the employees think about the implications of what the artists talk about as it relates to their work, the more they can envisage their own work growing to reflect the standards of class and style as discussed with the artists. Thinking, at Ferrari, is closely tied to doing. Precisely.

This emphasis on *thinking* brings us to our next insight, the first of three designed to help you and your company once a strategic initiative has already been launched. We're ready to discuss the most important things to do now that your team's work is under way. You've left port. You have ambitions and goals. You have a vision. You have mapped-out plans. *Now, how do you think about making it happen?*

Making it happen

Many people don't seem to be very interested in making things happen. It is often seen as a pedestrian task belonging to lower organization levels. The contributions from the top levels, too many believe, should rather be to formulate visions and strategies. Interestingly, for the last 200 years at least, social advancement has meant moving away from execution. Very often, we suggest to senior executives to review with us the next execution steps of their strategic initiative. We get the condescending message back that *we* don't seem to understand how things really work; the executive barks, 'You know, I have good people who do this for me. This is not what I am paid for! I have more important issues to think about.'

Well, the news we give to every executive is that 'making it happen' is precisely about thinking – *thinking through*. It is not about filling project spreadsheets and Gant charts. These are merely the written and communicable expressions of *thinking through* execution. You must translate a strategic initiative into execution phases, as we did when scoping the initiative. Then you translate each execution phase into sequenced activities. And then, you translate each activity into sequenced tasks. You should avoid, if at all possible, improvising when it comes to activities and tasks. Know where you're going and how you are going to get there. Follow this agenda:

Think it through

Imagine that you like gardening a lot. It's March, and you are attending a long and tedious business meeting. What are you thinking about? 'This year, I would really like to have a massive clump of roses next to the hedge. Oh, I need to stop at the store to get some fertilizer to prepare the soil. Where should I get the rose plants? But probably I should trim the hawthorn hedge first...'

While you are thinking through your garden project, you are *rehearsing mentally* each and every future step. You are rehearsing in your mind every option. You are rehearsing what could go wrong and what you could do about it. Mental rehearsal of a task fires many of the same connections in the brain that are used when you actually perform the task. For instance, it is well known that before a track event sprinters and hurdlers mentally envisage themselves running the course and rehearse every stride that they will take. And it's the same with all sports: archery, horse riding, skiing – you name it. It is part of building a 'can win' mindset.

Complex initiatives or projects are no different. Mental rehearsal of your next execution steps has several benefits:

Appraise

Many managers discover execution hurdles while mentally rehearsing the execution of the project. It is playing in your mind the movie of yourself executing the next steps. In this way, you reconnoitre the track and what it will take to jump each hurdle. But here's the key: when you are thinking about running the track, you need to envisage the hurdles and how you will leap over them. Bringing this back to a strategic initiative, if you mentally rehearse the execution of a task that requires parts that are scarce in the marketplace, for example, you can prepare to jump that hurdle *before* you are just in front of it.

Identify your options

You, of course, should be encouraging other members of your team to mentally rehearse as well; in particular, this can help the team prepare for any disruptions. By replaying the movie back with different scripts, you explore the 'what if?' scenarios and spot any hurdles far in advance. A plan will *never* unfold as planned. Mental rehearsal doesn't produce a plan, but it provides a web of options. This form of contingency planning is essential. In the heat of execution, having thought through your options ahead of time makes all the difference.

Create alignment

A third and less obvious benefit of mental rehearsal is that it creates team alignment and buy-in. Perhaps you do it alone for your garden, but for a strategic initiative it is much more effective to do it as a team. Everyone plays a role in rehearsing the next execution steps. Team members describe the script to each other. They challenge each other's script. They confront the unfolding story with disruptions. Progressively a shared scenario develops. Each team member knows exactly what is expected. The team is pretty confident that they can make it happen because they have already gone through it. Getting to the destination becomes a joint commitment.

Make mental rehearsal a team habit

Throughout execution, both the team leader and the sponsor need to be closely involved in mentally rehearsing the next steps. This is rather obvious for the team leader, perhaps less so for the sponsor.

The team leader should rehearse the next steps mentally with the team all the time. She does it before each large execution phase, each activity, each task. And she does it probably on a weekly basis whenever the team meets. Doing it often is the best way to build a robust execution roadmap. But because the team has its nose to the grindstone all the time, there can be issues that they don't see any longer.

So it is that the sponsor can also play a critical role in bringing a different perspective to the team's roadmap. Whenever he meets with the team, the sponsor can act as a sparring partner or sounding board. He challenges and 'sense checks' the team's thinking by asking questions such as: *What would it take to do this in two weeks less?* or *What is the worst thing that could happen to you during the roll out?* The role of the sponsor is to make sure that the team has left no stone – *no thought* – unturned (or no neuron untouched) during mental rehearsal.

Mental-rehearsal encounters between the team and the sponsor should not be occasional. How frequent they should be is a matter of judgement. The sponsor should sense how often this is needed. But a good team will seek these opportunities. Certainly, systematic mental rehearsal of the next execution steps is a habit to be developed.

Each of the four planning areas that we will now discuss requires mental rehearsal. These planning areas should not be seen as dry, mechanical tasks to be delegated to someone far lower on the organizational chart than you are. They involve a fair amount of trial-and-error thinking. You need to review feedback loops. You need to ask challenging 'what if?' questions. You need to replay the mental movie many times with different scripts. It is this mental rehearsal that will make the critical difference throughout the execution and, thus, will help move your strategic initiative towards a much higher probability of success.

Agile scheduling

Probably you are thinking, 'Mental rehearsal sounds good, but don't we also need detailed activity scheduling?' As the name indicates, activity scheduling consists in sequencing the activities to be performed, according to an input–output logic. Again, many people see this as an unexciting task for bean counters. It is time-consuming and requires discipline. Many people have fabricated smart rationalizations not to do it: 'No schedule ever works as scheduled; no plan ever works as planned. I will end up improvising anyway. So I might as well be practical and productive about it. I have enough experience to improvise.' We will show that agile activity scheduling is a smarter approach.

In addition to the fact that activity schedules are often treated superficially, they also generally suffer from three flaws that we want to address later in this section. First, however, let's focus on the need to include agility with your scheduling.

Schedule with agility

What we suggest is that, if you have mentally rehearsed your next steps, you will not need to improvise in response to disruptions. Mental rehearsal makes you acquainted with the terrain. It helps you identify which activities need to be frontloaded in your schedule. As we have seen, you should frontload learning-producing activities and cash flow-producing activities. And you should identify which activities you are not ready to commit to yet.

Then, you indulge in the detailed scheduling of the activities that you have frontloaded. You leave the others at the level of mental rehearsal (for the time being). Depending on the outcome of the activities that you have frontloaded, you will quite probably have to further rehearse mentally the later activities before you schedule them in detail.

The approach is tied to this question: 'What do I need to schedule *now*, and how do I monitor the rest?' We could describe all this as scheduling by successive approximation, going from the mental-rehearsal overview to the specific activity-schedule level. This is shown graphically in Figure 5.1:

◆ First, rehearse mentally the entire execution of the whole initiative. This covers all the phases outlined in the scoping. It is done first *as if* the execution context would only change in a predictable way. We know that this is quite likely to be a theoretical exercise. But it is helpful as a reconnaissance of the terrain and to prioritize the activities that must be frontloaded.

You prepare a high-level, *as-if* activity schedule for the whole initiative.

◆ The second step is to rehearse mentally, in more detail, the first execution phase – perhaps the second one also, if it makes sense. Don't commit further than you need to.

This should lead to a medium-level activity schedule for the first phase.

◆ As a next step, you rehearse mentally the first activities in the first phase, in full detail. Don't commit yet to what you don't need to commit to.

You have a fully detailed activity schedule of the first activities.

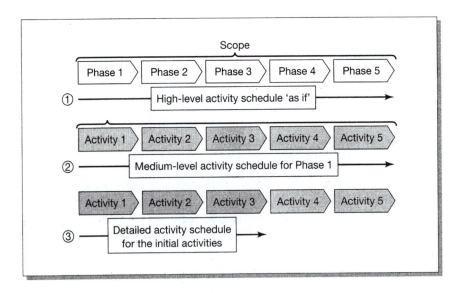

Figure 5.1 ◆ Scheduling by successive approximation

◆ As execution progresses, you move your detailed execution scheduling forward, always keeping your options open for as long as you can.

◆ As new knowledge is obtained from execution and as options are exercised, you need to update your high-level, *as-if* activity schedule. Execution priorities may evolve. This could lead you to reconsider some of the detailed activity schedules that you have already completed (but not yet executed).

All along, you need to keep in mind the value of mental rehearsal. This is not to get an immutable plan cast in concrete. It is to perform the terrain reconnaissance:

◆ To prepare your activity schedules for the time frame within which commitments need to be made

◆ To integrate new knowledge from earlier phases and activities

◆ To be able to respond effectively to disruptions by rescheduling activities according to your contingency options.

So, in summary, agile activity scheduling makes you focus on what you need to commit to, and helps you monitor the rest.

Set the deadline first

In conventional project planning, schedules are typically too long. Human nature is such that, when you ask how much time a certain task will take, people first consider how much work they already have on their plate. Then, mentally, they add the new task to their schedule. And then, to give themselves some margin, they add a little bit more time – as a kind of safety buffer to cover unexpected events or unexpected difficulties. Worse than this, when it comes to actually doing the work, they will probably start at the last possible moment. Even if the task is finished early, they are unlikely to make a special effort to deliver the output until on or around the deadline. The problem for the project manager is that everybody working on the project is doing the same thing. It's human nature. But it makes for long projects!

In practice, this means that it is much better to set the final deadline and then calculate backwards the steps required to reach it. This recommendation is widely known in operations management. By squeezing the project duration, you can attempt to eliminate extra 'dead' time in the schedule and stop everyone accumulating small safety buffers. But this will require a close cooperation with your providers of resources very early on.

Another way to bring the completion date forward is to ask yourself, for each scheduled activity, 'What is the earliest possible time this task can be started?' Sometimes you can improve the sequencing of activities. For instance, when a Nespresso team working on customer segmentation started to develop a detailed action plan, they initially planned each activity sequentially. Then, they realized that it would take more than four years to deliver any results! Following a review of the scheduled activities, the team realized that they could carry out several activities simultaneously. This cut the overall time to deliver by more than one year. See the example of 'Reson' below of how one company managed short-project cycles.

Reson

In 1995 Reson A/S, a company specializing in underwater acoustics and high-power electronics, needed to rethink how it managed the development of new products. Reson recognized that it had to reduce the new product development phase from three years to three months. It became clear to the Reson management that the company needed to fundamentally revise its approach to new product development.

To help shorten the project duration, project managers were given unlimited financial resources. Any costs could be incurred using internal or external resources. Claus R. Steenstrup, the managing director, explained:

> Unlimited trust is given to the project managers – they get the managing director's mandate for their projects. The only thing that matters is that the final deadline be met. This trust is based on the belief that when people are busy using their time constructively, when they know that all financial means are available, the actual costs are reduced. It is always possible for a single person to misuse the system, but in such a case, the person should be accused and replaced, not the system.

Any risks that jeopardized the final deadline had to be monitored. The smallest things might kill a project. A minor subcontractor in a low-risk area could be the highest risk. The company motivated its people to call in consultants to evaluate risks.

The company culture also needed to be developed. 'Culture', as Steenstrup saw it, meant 'the way to exchange ideas between people in an organization'. An example of Reson's new culture was 'free mobbing

Friday', initiated by employees in R&D and production. Every Friday, people in these departments were encouraged to share and discuss issues around collaboration with colleagues that might be blocking improvements.

Source: Reson: *Making Development Teams Accountable for Short Project Cycles*, Thomas E. Vollmann, Jussi Heikkila, IMD Case 6-0211, 1999

Set real targets

How often have you asked someone to perform a piece of work and then found that what you got back was not at all what you needed? How often have you had to debate whether a qualitative goal had been achieved or not?

Moreover, when the output of a task is sub-standard, you have to find a solution. Discussing the problem and finding a solution eats up valuable time. One option is that you decide to repeat the task with the hope of improving the output. Again, this costs precious time and resources. Perhaps you decide to invest additional resources to fix the problem. Then again, you may discover that you cannot truly fix the problem and are stuck with something sub-optimal that could put the whole initiative in jeopardy.

So, when you schedule activities, describe a specific quantified deliverable for each activity and each task. The key is to be as precise as possible about what the output will look like. Sometimes, the output cannot be measured in hard numbers but can be judged on a more qualitative basis. If so, find out who is the best judge and use their input to set the standards upfront before execution starts. To the question, 'Is the goal reached?', make sure that you can answer with a clear yes or no.

The buck stops where?

It is surprising how often it is difficult to identify who is accountable for delivering on a particular activity. Sometimes, it can be a whole department that is 'missing in action'. Often, larger activities seem to be shared among several persons, because they consist of several diverse tasks. It is very seductive to listen to people explain how, in *this* particular case, they will make this shared responsibility work out. Beware. The truth is that shared responsibility means that nobody is accountable.

The golden rule is that you should assign *one person* to be accountable for each activity. It does not matter if this person completes the activity directly or delegates it to other people. That particular activity is their responsibility and they are accountable. Single-point accountability means that you know whom to rely on during execution and who to keep on track. If there is a problem, then you know exactly who to call.

Scheduling resources

The availability of resources is always an issue during execution. Before we propose a simple resource-scheduling approach, we want to review three classical flaws that we have seen many times in our work: (1) too little, (2) too late, (3) not what you needed.

Resource needs are generally underestimated. They are not available when you need them. And they are not exactly what you needed for the initiative, which, by definition, follows new approaches.

Too little

An endemic problem of strategic initiatives is that teams systematically underestimate the resources needed to complete an initiative. Mostly this stems from a 'wait and see attitude'. As one manager complained to us, 'If we had really understood at the beginning of our strategic project what it would take in terms of people, resources and time, I'm not sure we would have gone ahead.' As discussed earlier, rehearsing the whole initiative mentally, as well as preparing an 'as-if' schedule, will help you anticipate these resources that are bottle-neck prone.

Too late

Teams have a kind of blind optimism that resources will be ready and waiting when they are needed. Then, when the deadline for the start of the activity comes around, they have to drop everything and scramble to find the resources.

In many cases, the team is asking for support from people who work in service departments, such as R&D or Marketing. Their budgets and schedules for the year are already fixed. By agreeing to help the team, these managers have to remove from the list other pieces of work and reallocate budgets. In many cases, they may not have the authority to do this.

Get early feedback from the people who will provide these resources. Then, make sure that these people have the time and budget to do the work.

The best advice that we can give is to start involving them as early as possible to secure the resources you need.

See 'Buying into critical milestones' below for the testimony of a team leader on this issue.

Buying into critical milestones

Our strategic initiative was to use our existing technological expertise to enter a new market segment in computer peripherals. As part of the initiative, we were assigned three technical resources in three different laboratories to complete the work.

At the start of the initiative, we set an aggressive schedule with the hope of having the first products ready within a year. At this time, we discussed our timeline with the three technical experts, and they appeared to agree with our forecast. However, as the technical work progressed, we realized that we had no hope of achieving our schedule. Each of these laboratory experts had far too much other work coming in from the other major business lines; and, because the three of them were working in different labs, coordination between them was difficult and extremely slow.

If I was to execute this initiative again?

- Firstly, I would insist on having all my technical resources in the same lab so that we would have critical mass.
- Secondly, I would make sure that these technical people could have a say in setting their own milestones.

What we found out from our experience was that, fundamentally, our critical milestones were not at all the same as their critical milestones. I think that if we had worked together to set the milestones at the beginning, even if this had meant having a longer time line, then they would have felt accountable for delivering.

Source: Product Line Manager, High-tech company

Not what you needed

With new strategic initiatives, some capabilities and routines that the organization has acquired in the past may no longer be compatible and may even prevent execution. Perhaps these bad habits used to be good habits in different contexts. But times have changed and now the organization needs to unlearn them. For example, we have seen an initiative get stuck because the sales force continued to sell using a low-price incentive. The new initiative called for the product to be sold at a premium. But the sales force never understood the major switch; it had been trained to sell products purely on a low-price sales pitch and was doing it very well – *too well* for the initiative!

We suggest four useful steps to identify the resources that you will need to execute your activity schedule.

Identify the critical resources

The first step is to recognize which resources are required by looking at each of the execution phases and activities, then listing what is needed to execute. To facilitate this task, we suggest thinking about resources in the four main categories outlined in the following table.

People	Systems	Infrastructure	Networks
◆ Knowledge	◆ Core processes	◆ Assets	◆ Customer networks
◆ Skills	◆ Support processes	◆ Locations	◆ Key accounts
◆ Experience	◆ Modes of operation	◆ Intellectual property	◆ Suppliers
◆ Mindsets	◆ Tools	◆ Brands	◆ Functional networks
◆ Leadership styles	◆ Organization structure	◆ Financial resources	◆ Best-practice networks
◆ Organizational values			◆ Employee networks
◆ Culture			◆ Community networks
			◆ Shareholders

Refer to the example of 'Opticom' to see how a company has assessed its required resources to double capacity in China. This list could become very long. You need to focus on the *most critical* resources. These are resources that are difficult to obtain and resources for which there is no work-around.

Opticom

Opticom makes custom-made optical components and sub-assemblies. The European company has manufacturing and assembly sites in Europe, USA and the Far East. Their largest customers manufacture electrical goods and are mostly located in the Far East. The company, once a niche player, has grown rapidly. A major challenge for Opticom is that the market for one of their core products is growing extremely fast. To maintain high market share, they will need to rapidly double production capacity in China. The team charged with executing this important strategic initiative analysed the critical capabilities that would be needed (see table, below). As a result, they realized that they had to add many more tasks to their operating plan!

People	Systems	Infrastructure	Networks
Training for key Chinese engineers in the USA (US Visas needed)	Qualification process of new machines in USA and China	Equipment for new production lines to be bought in USA, tested and imported into China	Customs clearing contacts for new equipment from USA
Chinese training consultant	New layout for the production process	Additional equipment for new production lines to be bought in China	
Operators for new lines	Improved production process to increase the quality of products from new line	Extension to changing room capacity for operators (legal requirement)	Network with Chinese recruiters
Chinese technical specialist for documentation			Network with Chinese recruiters associated with technical universities

Source: Disguised case

Assess their availability

Then, you need to assess the level of availability of the required resources. Are they:

♦ *Available?*
Is the resource available within the organization, or easily obtainable from the outside? For instance, schedule time in an R&D laboratory that has the skills and expertise to perform the task.

♦ *Missing?*
Your team needs to bring in or develop this resource. For instance, hire a salesperson skilled in selling a certain product.

♦ *Unrealistic?*
Sometimes your team may discover that a resource cannot be obtained. It does not exist in your organization. Or it cannot be acquired in time. Then, the only option is to go back to the drawing board and re-scope the initiative to make it achievable.

Mind the gap

The next step is to schedule *available* resources and to work on *missing* resources. These are activities to be added to your schedule. Scheduling *available* resources can still take time. Sourcing *missing* resources can often take longer than you might expect. In particular, the following capabilities are notoriously difficult and time-consuming: hiring new people, obtaining approvals for capital spending, negotiating deals, receiving regulatory approval and changing mindsets.

Financial resources warrant a special mention. The start of your strategic initiative is unlikely to coincide exactly with budget cycles. At least during the start-up phase, it is not always clear how the initiative will be funded.

Follow up

During execution, it is important to keep a close check on your resource schedule. Execution will certainly be re-routed more than once. You will learn from early execution phases. Disruptions will make your schedules unrealistic. So, you may have to re-align resources or access new resources.

As you can see, your resource schedule is not cast in concrete. It has to be adapted in real time to support an agile execution.

Check the instruments

Now, you have an agile activity schedule to execute the next phase of your initiative. You also have an agile resource schedule. But do you have an 'instrument panel' to monitor the execution?

The key performance drivers of your initiative are the factors that have most impact on whether your initiative delivers on its promised expected outcome. As we discussed earlier in the book, it's critically important to ascertain whether the initiative is delivering the promised *economic value*. The key performance drivers are the factors in your initiative that have most influence on the economic value it delivers. Thus, you need to identify and monitor these key performance drivers. But how? It is like deciding which gauges you want on your instrument panel in the vehicle you drive.

It is our experience that the key performance drivers of an initiative are rarely identified. At best, the team might verify that the economic value impact of the initiative is more than zero. At least, the team is happy if the initiative does not destroy value. Indeed, we have seen some teams enthusiastically execute initiatives that *have* destroyed value. We also saw some teams that spent months creating so little value that you wondered whether anyone truly knew the bottom-line impact of the initiative, especially those on the execution team! Two key points are important to stress in this regard:

Value calculation is not an exact science

Just as a reminder, the economic value created by your strategic initiative in a period of time is (more or less) the difference between its operating margin over that period of time – and the cost of the capital employed by the initiative in that same period of time. Some companies call it the *economic profit*.

A simple way to calculate the economic value created by your initiative over its life-cycle is to calculate the net present value (NPV) of the stream of cash flows it generates over its life cycle. Everyone is familiar with the NPV calculation. It is automated by all spreadsheet applications.

The calculation is straightforward. But, honestly, it doesn't say much. It is beset with uncertainties. A large and positive NPV can be mistakenly reassuring. Questions still arise such as: *How can we be sure what the revenues and costs will be five years from now? Who knows with any certainty what the assets will be worth at the end of five years? What about the intangible benefits that are not quantified on the spreadsheet? How do we factor the inherent risk of this initiative into our Weighted Average Cost of Capital (WACC)?* All of these concerns are valid. After all, none of us has a crystal ball to predict the future.

And in many cases an NPV calculation provides no clear right or wrong answer on whether to proceed. A good example is systems-installation initiatives such as CRM and SAP. For these initiatives, it is almost impossible to evaluate the level of improved efficiency and increased revenues that can be achieved. Yet, executives often argue that, without these unifying systems, the company will fall behind competitors who have already invested. As one of them confided to us, 'I guess it's like religion. You find out after you die whether you have landed in heaven or in purgatory!' He was an optimist.

The way to ensure that your business-based faith is not completely blind is to supplement any such calculation with managerial judgement. As a sponsor, you should gather reactions from other experienced people on the executive committee. Discussing such issues with the executive team will help them to make a judgement call in terms of the life expectancy of the initiative.

Now, if you apply the NPV approach to an agile execution schedule, you remove some of the medium- and long-term uncertainties in the calculation. It is no longer a one-time, all-or-nothing decision. You don't commit to any to-be-made-later decisions as long as you don't have to. You may stop the initiative *and still have created value*. If you decide to continue, it is on the basis of relatively more reliable and fresher data yielded by the most recent deliverables. But still, starting without being totally sure of the actual destination can make many people uncomfortable.

Know your value drivers

Once you have calculated the NPV of your initiative, the really interesting and relevant stuff is still to come. The next step is to find the key drivers of economic value using sensitivity analysis. This simply involves changing the main assumptions in your calculation and then looking at the impact on the NPV. For instance, if you have assumed that, because of your strategic initiative, sales will increase by 10 per cent and this yields an NPV of €20 million, then what would be the impact on the NPV if sales only increase by 8 per cent?

As you perform a sensitivity analysis, you will find that, if you vary some assumptions only slightly, they have a large impact on the bottom line. These are the *key drivers* of economic value for executing the strategic initiative.

Commonly, teams find that the NPV of the strategic initiative is extremely sensitive to the timing of deliverables. If you don't execute the initiative fast enough, then the revenues, or cost savings, from the initiative come far too late. They won't cover the initial investment outlay. The value of the initiative quickly turns negative.

There is even more to this observation. If the time-frame is shorter, then this reduces the risk of project failure. It reduces the uncertainty of the cash flows. For this reason, it is often better to add extra resources to an initiative and finish the project sooner. Fewer resources, and completing the initiative in a longer time, adds to the overall uncertainty of the initiative's success and is likely to eventually destroy value. Managers are often amazed at how strongly value creation is related to time. As one manager told us, 'I had never realized that, unless we get this project finished by the end of the year, we will have just wasted a lot of time and money!'

When you have the key financial drivers, you will be able to do three things:

◆ First, before even starting execution, the team can look for ways to improve its activity schedule.

   For instance, if you find out that your initiative is highly sensitive to time, then look for ways to complete the initiative faster, even if it means investing more resources. Or, if one of the key drivers is cost, then look for ways in which you can reduce the main cost elements.

◆ Secondly, now that you understand the key drivers, you know where to focus your attention during execution. If any of these key drivers start to slip, for any reason, then the team has to take immediate action.

◆ Thirdly, this sensitivity analysis gives you a valuable insight into what the main execution risks of your initiative are.

As you see, the real benefit from your economic value analysis comes when you perform the sensitivity analysis and identify your key performance drivers. See 'TRJ' below for an example of how this company used a sensitivity analysis to take a risky decision that saved it.

TRJ

TRJ is a designer of specialized computer systems for the automotive industry. The company essentially produces two products: *manufacturing systems* and *CRM systems*. The *manufacturing systems* business was very successful. The *CRM systems* business was proving to be problematic. TRJ had struggled to find a winning product. However, over the previous three years, it had developed a new *CRM system* called Auto-Update. The development team felt that Auto-Update was a winner. TRJ launched it in 2003; at first, sales were disappointing. Management decided to launch a strategic initiative to increase market share. The main goals of the initiative were to penetrate five big key accounts and sell 40 systems in 2004, rising to sales of 200 systems in 2007.

The team working on the initiative put together an NPV analysis of the initiative. They discovered to their horror that the NPV would be highly negative. Worse, even if they assumed that they could reduce the cost of building each Auto-Update system by 30 per cent, then the initiative would still not generate value. Moreover, if TRJ was to close the *CRM system* business entirely, then the *manufacturing systems* business would no longer be profitable because it would not be able to absorb the overhead. It was a crisis.

The team recognized that the key NPV financial driver was the number of Auto-Update systems that they could sell. Customer interviews highlighted that a major contributing factor to the low sales was its uncompetitive price. In a risky move, the team decided to drop the price of the new CRM system in the hope that this would lift the sales volumes. At the same time, the company pursued its strategy of entering key accounts. They also worked hard with suppliers to realize the 30 per cent cost reduction.

The gamble paid off. By the end of 2005, the number of CRM systems sold was much higher than expected. TRJ had secured large contracts at four of the big five key accounts. The product line was at last profitable.

Source: Disguised case

Manage execution risks

We have covered three areas of vital concern to anyone who is thinking while executing: activity scheduling, resource scheduling and monitoring key performance drivers. There is a fourth area to think about and it is major. Every initiative has critical execution risks that could potentially lead to the delay or failure of the whole project. This was clearly highlighted by the sensitivity analysis. For example, suppose the technology you are using to build a new product line might not be ready to install in your factories when you're ready to roll. Or suppose your key suppliers might be unwilling to negotiate price reductions. Or suppose the company that you want to acquire might not be interested in your offer.

If you don't identify these critical risks before execution starts, then you may be taken unawares once execution is under way. At that point, it may be too late for you to lessen the impact of the risk. You may find it impossible to put the strategic initiative back on track. However, if you understand these critical risks up front, then you can integrate tasks into your activity schedule to avoid the risk or at least to lessen its impact. You can also prepare contingency or fall-back activities that you can activate if the planned-for risk actually becomes a reality. To think about this, you need to ask some vital questions:

What are the risks?

The best way to identify these critical risks is for the team to start looking at the key drivers of economic value and brainstorm the risks associated with each driver. For instance, if a key driver is time, then ask the team to identify the risks that could delay tasks tied to the path of execution. Or, if a key driver is cost, then ask the team to identify the costs that could prove to be elastic, or ask the team to spot those costs that have a high probability of overrunning approved estimates. You need to identify any activities in which failure could derail the initiative, such as delicate negotiations with unions or joint venture partners that might go awry. *Any* potential showstopper should be considered.

What is the probability and impact of each risk?

From your team's list of risks, identify which ones have a high likelihood of occurring and could have a high impact on the outcome of the initiative. These are the critical ones. Investigate these critical risks further by asking:

- How can we reduce the probability of this risk happening?
- What are the early warning signals that we should look for?
- How can we reduce the impact of this risk?
- What should be our fall-back contingency plan if this risk occurs?

What can be done?

Now integrate tasks into your activity schedule to mitigate each risk. The list of critical risks should be seen as an 'evergreen' list. The team should continuously add newly identified risks. It should also delete the risks that they have successfully avoided.

How can we follow up to avoid surprises?

As each critical risk approaches, team members need to be obsessive about looking out for signs that the risk is occurring. There is no room for complacency. As soon as the team spots an early-warning signal, then it is time to activate plans to either prevent the risk from occurring or to reduce the impact of the risk once it has occurred. For certain risks, you will have no alternative but to dust down and activate contingency plans.

See 'German Packaging Equipment GmbH' below for an example of how this company factored its execution risks into its activity schedule, following a sensitivity analysis of the economic value of an initiative.

German Packaging Equipment GmbH

German Packaging Equipment GmbH was producing industrial packaging equipment. It was under huge price pressure in one of its most sophisticated packaging lines. It was about to launch an initiative to reduce the cost of goods sold of this packaging line by 25 per cent so as to increase its pricing flexibility.

Before embarking on the initiative, the team calculated the NPV of the initiative and performed a sensitivity analysis to identify the key financial drivers. On closer analysis, the team found that the risk of finishing the initiative behind schedule was much higher than the risk of not achieving the forecast cost reduction. In fact, if the team completed the year-long initiative as much as three months late, then the NPV would fall to zero. But if it only achieved a 20 per cent cost reduction, the NPV would be reduced to €15 million.

The team evaluated the execution risks for the initiative and plotted these risks in terms of their impact and probability. The team identified the four critical execution risks shown in the diagram below. As a result, they concluded that the initiative required active sponsorship (resources), clear governance (complexity), local business ownership (incentives), and a strong dimension of change management (acceptance).

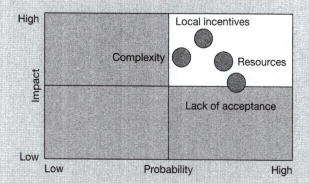

Source: Disguised case

All of the above insights should contribute to your effectiveness in developing agile execution schedules. However, you should keep in mind that there is no alternative to thinking through your execution ahead of time. With your team, you must rehearse mentally each and every step of it. With your team, you must simulate the flight of your initiative as it attempts to soar to success.

6

All aboard

ONE REASON TO BECOME passionate about strategic initiatives is that they can, literally, affect the life and death of your business. Consider MFI: starting from the original store, opened in 1964 in Edgware, Mullard Furniture Industries ultimately merged with ASDA in 1985 and grew to become a 200-store chain until it was sold to new owners in September 2006.[1] Its future is subject to question (the new owners bought the chain for one pound), but its past is something for us to note as we start to talk about the importance of getting everyone in your business behind the execution of your new initiative.

MFI, back in the 1980s, was a legendary retailer that received wide acclaim from students of management. No one caught their glory better than Walter Goldsmith and David Clutterbuck in their book written at that time, *The Winning Streak*. The authors recounted how, two days before the opening of a new store in Glasgow – and right during the busy holidays – the ribbon cutting was beset by serious flooding. With the store due to open on the first day after the holiday, top managers were understandably panicking. Goldsmith and Clutterbuck tell the story better than we can:

> *'The snow conditions were severe,' recalls an executive, 'with travel very difficult. It took [Managing Director] Derek Hunt himself thirteen hours to get there from London. Yet over a hundred volunteers came to help from all levels – managers, electricians, cleaners and warehousemen – from as*

---

[1] See webpage of the Centre for Retail Research
(http://www.retailresearch.org/reports/bust2007.php).

far away as London and Manchester. No one told them to come. They simply heard the news on the grapevine and made their way as fast and as best as they could. Eventually we had so many volunteers we were turning them away because we couldn't find enough for them to do.'[2]

Now, we ask you a pointed question: why don't we see more of this kind of behaviour in today's business world? One would hope that, in the last 30 years, great managers would have spawned great employees who, together, would have created legendary companies. Yet, as we said in our introductory comments to the book, it would seem that all the collected seeds of management wisdom have yielded relatively little business fruit. This is especially true with regard to the importance of getting everyone aboard your efforts to lead a strategic initiative.

A strategic initiative is entirely about leading people to a different way of conducting their business. Getting people excited about major change is a key challenge. If it is not addressed at the outset, any solution will fail – even if it was perfectly executed by the handful of people who planned the initiative. Who needs to be on board? To begin with, start with these three groups:

◆ Those who will have to change the most as a result of the initiative: your *target adopters*

◆ Those whom you will need to mobilize for resources required to execute the initiative: your *providers of resource*

◆ Those whose enthusiasm (or lack of it) will either support or hinder the execution of the initiative: *public opinion.*

But first, getting the above aboard will never succeed if you don't start with those at the very top of your organization.

Lead from the front

In many companies, the first reaction to the announcement of a strategic initiative is caution: 'Before we make up our mind to join, let's see what the party is all about.' In some companies, people may have even learned to be a bit cynical: 'Is the big change serious, *this time?*'

---

[2] Walter Goldsmith and David Clutterbuck, *The Winning Streak*, Weidenfeld & Nicolson, 1984.

To help win over such a wait-and-see attitude, it is first important that the top team is seen as fully committed to the initiative. The main indicator is contagious behaviour. Chiefs in battle used to be seen charging ahead – right towards the enemy – to rally their troops to follow, fired up by the same energy. The leaders' courage, back then, was convincing.

It is probably not as easy to be as convincing from the higher floors of your company's headquarters building. So, any other sign of commitment will be welcome. Courage at the top will naturally make most people *want* to emulate their leader's behaviour. They can see the kind of behaviour that is expected from them. They can make for themselves a mental representation of what they would want their own behaviour to look like.

Who should start 'the charge'? Of course, there is the initiative sponsor with the responsibility to make the initiative a success. But the initiative cannot simply be outsourced to the sponsor. The top team must agree to prioritize the initiative and be collectively determined to make it a success. All must relentlessly communicate its critical character, formally – through their presence, in their presentations, during speeches, by asking questions – as well as informally, with more subtle signals, such as encouraging comments, listening keenly to any details about the execution of the initiative and by attending major related events.

Another method is subliminal communication. Any hesitation about executing an initiative from one of the members of the top team will be seen immediately by others and amplified rapidly. This is because people are all watching for signals of what to do.

A quick story: an important financial analysts' event was taking place on the very day that the leader of a huge initiative was presenting his roll-out plan to the company's country heads. None of the executive-board members could be present because they were attending the analysts' event.[3] The word got around that the initiative did not really have the full support of top management. The slight was not intentional, but top management made sure that the same situation did not happen next time. At the next progress-review meeting with the country heads, 18 months later, the whole executive board was sitting in the first row.

It is in fact very easy to signal that an initiative doesn't have to be taken too seriously, through silences, omissions, jokes: 'Oh yes, the initiative! I almost forgot...' The slightest sign that could be interpreted as a hesitation

---

[3] Nestlé's Globe Program (C): 'Globe Day', Peter Killing, IMD case 3-1336, 2005.

within the top team will be enthusiastically gossiped about across the organization. The credibility of the initiative will be undermined. The mobilization across organizational silos will be more difficult. And the execution team's energy will be affected by perceived or real political issues. Legitimate differences of views at the top need to be settled ahead of going public. When the top supports a strategic initiative, it must totally support it.

We recall a corporate moment when this was emphatically *not* the case. It was the first plenary meeting of all the teams involved in launching a set of strategic initiatives. The teams were sitting at different tables and the members of the top team had been spread among them. The CEO was doing his best to share his own enthusiasm with the audience and he was doing a great job. But one of his colleagues from the top team was sitting sideways, almost turning his back to his table, and at some distance from it. His physical posture was signalling aloofness. Occasionally, he was glancing at his PDA to check whether any email had arrived.

The effect was simply disastrous. Sitting there quietly, doing almost nothing, he had more impact than the CEO's best efforts to instil energy. What do you think was going through the minds of the people sitting around? Signalling the importance of something requires *active* signalling, *conscious* signalling. Beware of unintentional bad signalling.

It is also important for the top team to realize how much time will be needed from them if they want to provide necessary guidance, and if they don't want to be perceived as focusing on something else. In a conversation with the CEO of a company about to launch a number of critical initiatives, we asked: 'Do you realize that these initiatives will require about 60 per cent of your top team's time for the next eight to ten months?'

'But this is not possible!' was the CEO's response. Yes, it probably *was* impossible. A pre-selection process of the initiatives was introduced to eventually increase the focus on fewer of them, but the senior managers also had to think about what they could delegate.

Victims of success

Strategic initiatives propose and implement changes on behalf of the whole organization. There are many on the receiving end, within the organization, whose mode of operation will be changed. We refer to these 'beneficiaries' and 'victims' as the *target adopters* of the initiative. At the outset, they often don't know that the initiative is meant to help them.

Some people, for example, will have to sell, service, support and install new products or services. They need to understand what the business logic of these changes is. Some people may be expected to run their local business quite differently, following the introduction of a new CRM, or of a re-engineered supply chain, decided by the managers launching the initiative. Some initiatives require the adoption of a corporate-wide, standardized process, replacing local processes that local people had got used to. It is likely that many will be surprised by all the new operating standards.

In many instances, the target adopters are handed a *fait accompli*. They are brought into the picture after the fact, when told to change or when trained to use the new approach. How many SAPs or CRMs are implemented as IT projects by IT people, rather than as business projects by business managers? Perhaps, technically, the initiative will work. But the target adopters will not be on board. They will see no compelling local business reason for adopting this centrally driven change. The team must address some fundamental questions:

What's in it for us?

The point is that the target adopters will easily see the pain of change that is being imposed upon them. They will less easily see the benefits of change. They know that someone up top wants the initiative to happen. What is in it for them is less clear. Getting the target adopters to endorse the initiative is not achieved top–down: 'Here is the new way in which you should work: isn't it great? Comply.' Little will happen if the target adopters do not understand, welcome and endorse the changes. You need to have the target adopters aboard before you leave the port. There will be very little chance for a second call.

Many initiatives, for example, will aspire to replace locally designed processes by globally standardized ones deemed to increase the overall corporate competitiveness.

For example, a technology firm, seeing that customer-perceived value was rapidly shifting from systems to solutions, launched an initiative to develop professional services capabilities to design and sell business solutions. Local sales forces were to change to business consultants.

Senior local managers were not enthusiastic. They had already been doing their best to respond to their local business conditions. The 'new way' was dictated to all from a distant manager at headquarters. Local managers were questioning whether this unproven approach was really a priority. They had a local business to run with targets to achieve. 'Selling solutions' sounded like a costly distraction.

Sales forces were divided. The more experienced sales people were worried that they could not adapt to becoming business consultants. Some saw all this talking about selling solutions as criticism of how they were achieving their target figures. On the other hand, the younger sales people, interested in the change, were making contact directly with headquarters to see how they could be part of the new game – creating even more resentment from their bosses.

This soon resulted in overt conflict. Legitimate questions from the local heads were perceived as resistance to change. And everything from headquarters was suspect to the local heads – this initiative or any other. The reaction, as is often the case, was to organize more meetings and to deliver more presentations to depict the great future.

But more PowerPoint® will never fix this kind of problem. This was putting the cart before the horse. The target adopters should be at the starting point of the initiative, not at its ending point. It is generally helpful to assume that they are trying to perform locally as well as possible. They need to see how the initiative will help them do so. They need to see themselves on the winning side, not on the victim's side. This is easier when a culture that finds it advantageous to share information already exists, rather than a culture where it is preferable to keep to oneself. When the 'not-invented-here' ideas have proved helpful in the past, there is more openness to shared solutions.

Who's driving the initiative?

The benefits from the initiative have to materialize locally. Local management must see the benefits of running their local business more effectively as well as not having to perform tasks that can be done more effectively elsewhere. Understanding the local business benefits of a centrally led initiative will have to be a bottom-up process.

It must start with a business-issue analysis that is conducted with the target adopters, by the target adopters, so that they bring forth what they expect from the initiative. They may well be the experts on the issues to be addressed. Their inputs are needed to assess the current situation. They have a view on what the root causes of problems are, which may differ from that of the centre. Their inputs are needed to prioritize execution so that tangible local benefits are obtained as fast as possible and tested. Their inputs are needed to get feedback on execution. And they provide the final sign-off.

The turning point of getting the target adopters aboard is when they find that they are being listened to and that they can have a say in designing the outcome of the initiative. They need to prove that they can perform better when given a chance. They need to retain some control over the way they conduct their business. They need to feel part of the winning team that stands behind a dynamic corporation. First-hand experience is, of course, essential in achieving this mental turning point. Success stories from other units, testimonials from peers, public recognition for a successful roll-out, promoting best practices across the organization – these are all also effective ways to bring target adopters aboard.

How can we help?

To achieve this endorsement right from the start, target adopters should also be represented in the core team. Or they should be part of a steering group. And they must be fully fledged members of execution pilots. This will allow them to see how the big picture also serves their local business interests, and how the overall initiative can also be a local initiative with local business benefits. This will also allow them to localize the overall message in a way that focuses on concrete local benefits, not just on the top–down execution of the headquarters' 'smart ideas'.

Getting and keeping people aboard when the outcome of an initiative is as dramatic as a closure is also important. In such situations people will feel threatened and they will respond in kind when they feel badly treated. A software firm was transferring much of its code writing to India. This could not be achieved successfully without the cooperation of the very people who were losing their jobs. That's not easy to do.

Another case in point: a consumer goods company was closing a plant in a small town in the USA. Not only did it need the plant output until its last day, but it did not want to leave behind a bitter taste that could make the news and hurt its reputation. Getting people to say nice things ('It'll work out alright. We get good support writing a professional résumé and looking for a new job, and a good severance package that includes financial assistance during retraining. So I've no complaints – I just wish it wasn't happening.') kept them aboard even beyond the separation.

Getting your target adopters aboard is not achieved overnight. It requires time to allow them to move through the mental stages of going through change: denial, anger, bargaining, depression and acceptance.[4] The same

---

[4] This sequence is known as the Kübler-Ross Grief Cycle. As discussed in Chapter 1, *Focus First*, it was initially developed to describe how patients respond to their condition.

two-way communication must be maintained, consistently over time. The same quality of first-hand and emotional experience must be maintained throughout execution.

Resource poachers

Strategic initiatives, by definition, don't have permanent resources. As discussed before, the idea is to redeploy resources flexibly from across the organization to apply them to a strategic priority that none of the silos can address alone. So, strategic initiatives need to go poaching for resources.

Mobilizing the owners of resources is an organizational challenge. Those at the top who first blessed the initiative should, to be sure, help to fund it. But, later, you will also need specialized resources from different functions: information technology, R&D, marketing – or from business-unit or country heads. And you will need funding. This requires preparation, planning, coordination, just to make sure that the resources are available in time. Here are the best ways to think about this challenge.

Strategic initiatives are an *organizational* challenge

Because they don't have a permanent organizational structure, strategic initiatives are a challenge to well-structured corporations. They don't easily fit with neatly organized silos and processes. These silos and processes are all justified by productivity considerations, and they do their job as well as possible. But, in doing so, they get in the way of strategic initiatives. Strategic initiatives require a cross-organization alignment that is not natural to these organizations.

The resources you need to access are not idle, waiting to be used. Most certainly, they are currently being used productively. They are in finite quantities. When applied to a task, they are not available for other tasks. And they are assigned according to rigorous yearly processes through which their use has had to be justified. They were probably not easy to acquire.

By contrast, strategic initiatives are launched without specific reference to the same yearly budgeting calendar. The silos from which resources are being poached have to change their priorities. Many organizations do not know how to handle these disruptions.

Designing more flexible processes is part of the answer. It must be built into the mindsets that silos don't own resources. They hold them on behalf of the whole organization. And resources can be redeployed as needed. Otherwise, there is no hope for strategic initiatives to ever work.

Reprioritization, time allocation and performance management are the three most frequent sources of frustration when tapping cross-organizational resources.

What will not be done

When a strategic initiative is prioritized, there is a need for a process to reprioritize previous decisions and decide what will *not* be done or what will be done later.

Funding the initiative is a case in point. We have seen initiatives being launched without giving any attention to where the money was going to come from. For example, seed money will be required at least until it has been demonstrated that the initiative generates economic value. Whose budget is it going to come from? In many companies, headquarters routinely makes demands from local units that require the assignment of significant local resources. It is often assumed that the same creeping process can be used to fund large initiatives. But it is unlikely that this will raise much local support and enthusiasm for the initiative. As obvious as it may sound, a dedicated funding mechanism must be provided as soon as the initiative is decided.

Your initiative will also need specialized functional resources, for example from development labs, from IT, from marketing, and possibly resources from country units. These organizational units have established their resource requirements on the basis of the requests they recieved from various business units, across the organization. Now comes the initiative, threatening the continuation of previous projects or of ongoing tasks. If resources are applied to the initiative, something else will not be done. Some other units will not receive the support they were counting on.

These choices are often swept under the carpet, hoping for the best. Many organizations believe in miracles and expect that everything will more or less work out in the end. When launching a new initiative, senior managers tend to be over-optimistic – with annoying resource requirements.

Resource requirements will not go away. It is critical to be upfront in facing this reality. Choices have to be made: what will be done and what will not be done? Again, if a strategic initiative is prioritized, other activities must be de-prioritized. This must be communicated early on, rather than left as a surprise for victims who are genuinely pursuing what they had committed to in due time.

Some flexibility must also be built into resource-allocation processes. Not everything will get done at once. A resource-allocation plan should be seen as a list of prioritized options, not as an untouchable entitlement for the next 12 months. In a fast changing environment, these options may have to be reprioritized, removing and adding projects, as more information becomes available.

Time allocation

The team leader does not only have to negotiate with the line bosses of each of his team members, to squeeze time out. She also has to address this same issue with the line bosses who formally supervise the execution team members who will be expected to contribute specialized capabilities for specific periods of time. Otherwise, playing musical chairs across projects will be disastrous. Yet, this is what happens in many organizations that venture to launch strategic initiatives without having ensured that the underlying processes will support it.

A story to illustrate: Ralf, the head of IT, has carefully planned the assignments of his team members with several other unit heads to complete the projects he has committed to deliver to them. Now, he has to go back to them and explain that, because of the strategic initiative, their projects will be delayed.

Clearly, this shouldn't just be Ralf's problem. In organizations that believe that strategic initiatives are an effective way to address selected priorities, job assignments cannot be seen as an entitlement. HR processes need to pay attention to it in advance. All need to expect that the best people will soon get an opportunity to take up a new challenge. Their rapid replacement, if required, should have been thought out in advance.

As for core team members, assignments to extended teams should not be treated as opportunistic decisions, but as part of individual development plans. It is known in advance that, should an opportunity occur, one may have to drop some of one's tasks to move on to the next assignment. In strategic-initiative-smart companies, contingency plans are already in place when an initiative is decided.

Performance management

The strategic-initiative team leader also has to make sure that the performance-management targets of all those involved are not at odds with the needs of the initiative.

In many organizations, not only the core team members – but also the extended-team members – find themselves torn between their team assignment and their 'day job'. If they spend time on the former, they will have to sacrifice some aspect of the latter. Perhaps, the system of performance and reward on the initiative team is not even clear yet – but what is clear is that their 'day job' performance will suffer. Enough flexibility in the performance-management processes must have been designed right from the start, even before strategic initiatives are considered. From a long-term perspective, reward systems also need to rely significantly on the overall corporate performance, rather than reinforcing parochial interests.

Take them to heart

Providers of resources, capabilities and know-how must also see themselves as members of the extended team, as members of the team for a specific contribution at a specific point in time. As members of the extended team, their commitment will be triggered by the same motives as core-team members and as target adopters. First, they want to prove themselves by being part of the initiative challenge and they expect recognition for this. Second, they resent a solution being imposed on them as if they were just a commodity that can be used any time, anywhere. Third, they want to be treated as members of the initiative team.

These three motives for committing explain why it is so important for providers of resources to be associated early on in designing the solutions through which the initiative will be executed. By contrast, as we have witnessed (sadly) too many times, the most effective way to make their support lukewarm is to treat them as a utility that can be plugged in at a whim. An example of the positive effect of involving the providers of resources is described opposite in 'Mobilizing through the right person – a team leader's story.'

Winning public opinion

Let us define the challenge tied to public opinion by relating a situation we once observed. A service company we know was still in a state of shock. Everyone had become accustomed to strong performance. But, then, it had had to issue a profit warning because of bad cost overruns in some projects and rapidly increasing low-cost competition in some activities. Strong

Mobilizing through the right person – a team leader's story

Our initiative was a corporate-growth initiative. To execute it, we had to borrow resources from another business group. One important resource that we needed at various points in the execution plan was laboratory testing of the lead compounds in the formulation.

At the start of the project, we relied on country people to coordinate with the laboratories to get this done. Coordination attempts were not very successful, leading to substantial delays and backlogs. So to improve the situation, I personally negotiated directly with all laboratory heads and asked them to commit to a more rapid turnaround time. We also created an innovation group including core team members and the individual application scientists. This group then met regularly to decide on which leads they should test and in what application.

Since then, turnaround time and commitment from the laboratories has improved significantly. I think that I can attribute this change to two things. Firstly, when the laboratory heads agreed to prioritize our work, this sent a strong signal to the people under them who had to perform the analyses. Secondly, involving these people in the decision-making process helped to generate commitment and buy-in.

Source: R&D business line manager, specialty chemicals company

cost-containment measures were being implemented. An initiative was also being launched to refocus the activities on some key segments less exposed to low-cost competition. But the initial shock about the setback in profit flow (which seemed like failure) was still working its way through the system: some of the service company's best people were already leaving. It was critical to accompany the initiative with a communication plan to take people's minds off the deadly internal focus on failure and back to the fighting spirit and entrepreneurship that had made it successful.

In this case, and many others, public opinion within the organization matters. You want it to support the strategic initiatives. Many people have opinions on what is going on and influence others in ways that can undermine your most critical initiatives. You cannot leave the public opinion in your company to be shaped by the chatter heard at the locations of the coffee machines.

Actively maintaining a positive buzz is necessary to keep the focus on strategic priorities, to dispel false interpretations, and, mostly, because the alternative is silence, which can be grossly misread. Silence around strategic initiatives is deadly: human minds naturally suspect the worst when they are not kept informed and reinforced with positive news. A positive buzz supports the success flywheel and helps maintain the execution energy. The people involved feel good. Others predictably want to help.

A strategic initiative produces ripples across the organization. Some people will feel negatively affected, not only your target adopters, but also people whose plans are delayed or changed. They need to see that, overall, the initiative will make the whole organization more successful.

In any organization, there are opinion leaders. They may have nothing to do with the initiative. But you want their support because they can mobilize – or demobilize – others whose support you need. Keeping a positive buzz covers the whole spectrum, from leveraging the energy, to damage control. To get on top of all this, ask the following questions:

Who are the opinion leaders?

Their number is generally underestimated. Some have large audiences and may influence a large part of the organization. Others have smaller audiences and may influence a small but critical part of the organization, such as one providing a critical resource.

Opinion leaders may overlap with the previous constituencies we have discussed: target adopters and providers of resources. This makes it even more important to monitor where they stand.

We propose displaying them on a map similar to a risk-assessment map: according to their level of agreement with the initiative and to their level of impact on the initiative.[5]

Level of agreement

To what extent does one agree with the expected outcome of the initiative and with the execution approach? Initiatives do attract interest and people take positions. It is not always easy to assess where they stand.

---

[5] The first person whom we saw use this map was Jean-Marie Descarpentries, a master change leader with an exceptional turnaround record.

Level of impact

To what extent can one facilitate the execution of the initiative, or hinder it? Sources of influence may come from hierarchical power over people involved in the initiative, personal influence through relationships and social networks, and as gatekeepers who can control access to information and resources. But people at lower organization levels may also control the availability of critical resources.

You can then identify four main groups among opinion leaders (Figure 6.1), with different likely behaviours. Of course, the boundaries between the groups are fuzzy. This is just a rough cut of how people may respond to the initiative. But, overall, you will have to approach them differently, with different communication strategies to reinforce, modify or neutralize their behaviours.

How do we manage everyone?

Your 'supporters' need attention

They feel good to you. They agree and they can help. But you need to assess their motives to understand how robust their position is. Do they agree for the right reasons? Will they use their potential impact, or is it just words?

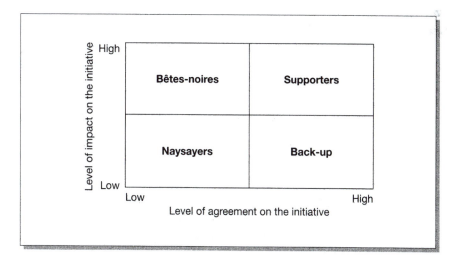

Figure 6.1 ◆ Mapping your opinion leaders

Because you do not expect any trouble from them, there is a tendency to take them for granted – or to talk to them only when they are needed. It is important to keep in contact to steer their support. You need to decide, and agree with them, in what capacity they can best help the initiative.

It is also important that you keep in contact with them to inform them of your progress. To be able to help you, they need to know what is going on.

Giving due recognition to their support is also helpful, not only to keep them aboard, but also to bring in more people. Ungratefulness doesn't attract support.

Your 'bêtes noires' need even more attention

These people are a substantial concern for you. You see them as 'bêtes noires', an ill omen. You see them as the internal enemies. There is often a tendency to avoid them just because they disagree. But they have impact. Probably a negative impact at the moment, but, if it could be redirected to support the initiative, this possibility should not be foregone.

In fact, either as the initiative sponsor, or as the team leader, you should really be doing your best to keep in contact with them. You need to understand why they disagree. What do they see that you don't see? Is this not the right priority? Is this not the right time? Is this not the right approach? They may well be a source of valuable information on what could go wrong and why.

By discussing openly with them, by listening to them, you could improve your approach, benefit from their insights, address their concerns and dispel misunderstandings. You could win their agreement and benefit from their support. Or you could agree to disagree and obtain their neutrality. At a minimum, you will know what the opposition thinks ahead of anyone else.

Your 'back-ups' can be mobilized

These are people who agree, but can't do much for you. They can be seen as nice-to-have allies but of no consequence. Such an opinion is a mistake. Their impact could be increased. This is the reason why we call them 'back-up'.

One project leader finding that country heads were slow in providing their support started talking with the people one or two levels below. There, he found impatient subordinates who had been waiting for change for a long time; they agreed that this new initiative was the right way to go. They had even secretly tested some of the ideas. And they had views on how to go further, faster. Seeing that they would get support from the initiative, they started to create pressure from below.

Where are your hidden resources? Where can you find people looking for change? Who knows best what needs fixing, with no axe to grind? Who has little to lose and much to gain in changing the status quo? Where are your execution experts – closer to the frontline, or sitting in the head office? Keep addressing such concerns.

Your 'naysayers' are probably best ignored

They disagree and their nuisance power is to talk. Because they can't do much, they talk. It is always irritating to see people disagree and this may unnecessarily occupy your mind. But winning the initiative battle is not a popularity contest. You want the initiative to succeed. Don't waste your energy where it does not matter.

There might be some prominent players in this group, or people whom you trust and respect who, for some reason or other, have grave concerns about the initiative. You need to talk to them selectively to find out why they disagree. As with your 'bêtes noires' they may know something that you have missed and they could be a good source of information on potential problems.

You may also find there is a very fragmented opposition of people who are dissatisfied with the initiative for a variety of reasons – or perhaps just dissatisfied with anything. You probably don't need to lose sleep over them. Proffering more facts and results to uninformed idlers will not get you many new votes of support. It could just tickle the fighting spirit of the supporters of the initiative.

Just beware of a coalition built on inertia. It is easy to underestimate because it is not very visible. But it can sink an initiative. Responding fast to naysayers, for example by emphasizing successes, is often a way to reduce the membership of your opposition, bit by bit.

How do we communicate effectively?

In addition to the constituencies that we have discussed in this chapter – your target adopters, your providers of resources, and your opinion leaders – it is also important that you maintain a supportive buzz for your initiative across the organization and beyond. There are several reasons for this.

One is that silence is always bad. For most people in an organization, no news is bad news. A well-publicized launch followed by official silence will trigger all sorts of suspicions and eventually undermine cooperation. But, also, silence will suggest that the initiative is not an appropriate conversation topic, and this will suppress your getting useful feedback. 'The Secret Initiative', below, provides an example of the consequences of keeping your initiatives underground.

The secret initiative

In 2001, a large US high-tech company announced a major growth initiative consisting of 12 separate growth projects divided into new product lines and new geographic regions. The CEO launched the growth initiative himself. His opening speech was widely published in the press and talked about by investment analysts.

After the initial launch, the CEO and his executive board became very nervous about releasing any specific details of the projects, fearing that their competitors would also follow them into the same product areas or would try to lure away key managers who were running these projects. As a result, very little information was released about the strategic initiative, even within the company (not even information of a general nature).

A year later, the project leaders of these 12 projects were perplexed and unhappy. The company had asked them to work on a high-profile initiative that was now effectively a secret. One leader complained, 'I'm finding it very difficult to get support for my project. Everyone seems to be so cynical about the growth initiative, and the number of cynics seems to have drastically increased over the last few months. We are just not able to mobilize people to support the initiative. I know that the CEO has discontinued some of the projects, but nobody has communicated the reasons for this to the organization; and this also leads people to the conclusion that the growth initiative is just not important for our business. The initiative was supposed to mobilize the whole company; but instead, it has just faded away.'

Another project leader commented, 'We need to let employees know about the projects and report our progress. We need active periodical exposure of selected projects to the organization and especially to senior managers. This is the only way we will get the support we need.'

Source: Disguised case

Another reason for open communication is to engender widespread support. This is an obvious thing to do when the news is good and the initiative is making progress. Everyone wants to be associated with success. But it is also true when difficulties ensue. They must be acknowledged.

Communicating relentlessly across the whole organization on the initiative is not optional. You need to describe time and again where the initiative fits in the strategic big picture. You need to repeat why it is high priority. You need to depict endlessly what its expected outcome is. You need to explain unremittingly which changes will have to take place. And when you think that you are done, you need to start over again.

People across the organization also want to know how the initiative will function, how it will be organized, who will do what. People will also want to know what the consequences of the initiative will be for them, how they will be affected, what is in it for them. A good example of addressing this concern can be found in an internal booklet that was published by the Finnish stainless steel producer, Outokumpu, when it launched a major operational-excellence initiative, OK – 1 (see below).

Outokumpu: becoming the world's 'Number One'

In 2005, CEO Juha Rantanen set for Outokumpu the goal of becoming the number one stainless-steel producer in Europe within three years, and the number one globally within five years.

To support this goal, two excellence programmes were launched: OK–1, a production excellence programme, and K2, a commercial excellence programme. This was a new approach for a rather traditional company. It signified a significant change of culture towards more openness and the will to address issues as 'one company'.

To support the kick-off of OK–1, Outokumpu launched a communications campaign intended to make it clear that things were changing. In particular, a pocket-size booklet was issued to each employee: 'OK–1 Becoming the World's Number One.' Its purpose was to explain what OK–1 was all about, using a list of 13 frequently asked questions, one per page. Each response was supported by a cartoon depicting a team of puppy soccer players on their way to winning the cup. The cleverness of the communications campaign caught on throughout Outokumpu, which rallied to the goals.

- What is OK–1?
- Why OK–1?
- What's wrong with the way we used to do things?
- Who does OK–1 apply to?
- How will OK–1 be put into effect?
- What's OK–1 got to do with me?
- Where are we headed?
- How is OK–1 organized?
- Okay, so what's next?
- What happens after kick-off?
- When will OK–1 be complete?
- What's in it for me?
- Where can I get more information about OK–1?

Source: Outokumpu

People will always want to know whether the initiative is making progress – or whether it is encountering difficulties. People want to know whether the important milestones are being reached, whether the pilots have been successful. It is critical that you quench this thirst for knowledge.

How do we keep the buzz going?

Communicating at this level helps people understand the value of the strategic initiative from a rational perspective – what we're doing makes sense and it will improve our market position. But it also creates an emotional bond between everyone in the organization and the initiative. This bond has a halo effect beyond the initiative itself. It sustains organizational energy. Success stories contribute to the success flywheel. When there are few tangible results to show (that is, bottom-line results), stories of

What's OK–1 got to do with me?

Use your head! Let's put our best practices and right methods to work. To learn from them calls for sharing information. You'll see that as OK–1 moves forward piece by piece, it will affect the whole of Outokumpu, you included. How it does this is something you can yourself influence. Changes will be made that will improve machinery and equipment utilization, work methods, occupational safety, and materials management, based on measurements. These changes will also enhance the working environment by improving tidiness and good order.

There's no need to invent the wheel again in dozens of places because OK–1 will pass on the best practices to all of us. By sharing what you know, based on your experience and observations, you will be creating the keys to success for Outokumpu. And that works the other way too: be prepared to change the way you work and the methods you use when you learn of something better. OK–1 will provide training, dialogue and information for this purpose.

breakthroughs in the lab, of customer feedback or of major local adoptions help keep the buzz going. It will contribute to bringing aboard your target adopters and resource providers.

Sharing this information with the organization at large also contributes to giving public recognition to the team. As a sponsor, or as a team leader, you know that it helps sustain the team's energy. At the same time, it makes the team's commitment public and it raises the bar.

Some companies involve their internal communications department from the start and resort to a range of different media for different occasions. For example, to support its initiative 'Cascading leadership principles and behaviours', Outokumpu developed a game board that made people discuss how the company's leadership principles applied to the different situations found along the game track. The company also developed a video in which the CEO interacted with cartoon characters in situations exemplifying the principles. At first, many people were shocked by such 'PR techniques'. But it certainly caught everyone's attention. And the younger organization members thought this was a 'cool' way for the CEO to communicate these principles.

Communicating on your initiative is a never-ending job. It needs repeating and repeating. A sustained communication plan must be prepared right from the start, not as an afterthought or as a reactive measure. People across the organization need this continuity and consistency to adjust mentally to this overarching priority that supersedes all silos.

Back in the 1980s, those leading MFI had to be doing something right. In a crisis tied to the opening of a new and important store, 100 employees fought floods and snow to enssure that the strategic initiative happened – *without being asked to do so*. This means that 100 people, quite probably remote from those who would operate the store when it opened for business, were on board with the importance of making sure the initiative did not die prematurely. No company could ask for more; no company needs any less.

Your strategic initiative is meant to have an impact on people. It is meant to change the way they run the business. It is not meant to deploy processes, organization set-ups or even new technologies. These are means, not ends. The people on whom you want to have an impact and whom you want to change are your target audience. You need to *start from* them, not end with them.

7

Follow through

IN MARCH 2007, the CNBC European Business network broadcast its 'Innovation Issue.' In all, 50 'key innovators' were heralded for their inventiveness. The survey, CNBC said, was carried out in a rigorous fashion: 'On behalf of CNBC European Business, strategy consultants PRTM surveyed 60 companies over a two-year period using around 150 product development metrics to identify specific levers for product and service innovation.' Without doubt, you would recognize some of the company names. Constantin (Germany), Aresa A/S (Denmark), Industria (Iceland), Inditex (Spain), ABB (Switzerland), Tesco (UK) – the list is impressive.

To win a spot on the list, companies were interviewed extensively. PRTM said that each candidate was grilled using a questionnaire that included 150 questions and over 500 data points. But we raise this list of innovation Olympians to make a point that is central to this, our final insight in this book. These 50 companies were spotlighted because they came up with, in some cases, most engaging ideas for improving their position in the market-place (for example, Royal Bank of Scotland appointed a chief innovations officer!). Yet, it is the explanation of what was *really* required to be named a 'key innovator' that stole our attention. Here's what CNBC European Business said:

> *Put simply, great ideas are worthless on their own. The key to success is the development and delivery of the idea in the form of a novel product that customers will pay for. Ideas need to be filtered to separate the valuable from the merely clever, then separately funded through the delicate concept phase, where a 'not invented here' attitude can kill them off. Product*

development teams must then be chartered to develop revenue-generating products, bringing together design, technologies, market creation, sales and volume delivery capabilities to turn the ideas into winners.[1]

Aha! As we said at the very beginning of this book, having a great idea is simply not sufficient to execute a strategic initiative. After the new idea takes root among the members of the executive team, after the concept has been fleshed out with conceptual mapping, after the initiative has been adequately resourced, after all the key players are fully on board with the roll-out – after all is said, *something has to be done – and carried to full completion.*

Follow-through is carrying out an intention or project until its full completion. Everyone readily agrees that follow-up is important – but nobody likes it. Follow-up verifies that a target has been achieved. Follow-through is concerned with what to do next – until the initiative is a functioning reality. Without follow-through, follow-up is of limited use. It may even be frustrating.

Indeed, follow-up alone can easily be experienced as sheer control that something has happened or not. Many people on the receiving end of follow-up perceive it as an almost 'criminal investigation' meant to uncover their wrongdoings. It often consists in looking for the culprits and finding out whose fault it is to have someone to blame – even though blaming has never fixed a bad situation. There is a perceived likelihood that follow-up will end up with some form of punishment.

Many managers readily admit that they don't like doing follow-up and, thus, end up not doing any at all. We often hear offended responses like 'I trust my people! So I can focus on matters other than follow-up!' Many managers rationalize their shying away from follow-up by suggesting that they do not want to intrude and be perceived as distrustful micromanagers. We suggest that this is because they never tried follow-through. Yet, *execution is all about follow-through.*

---

[1] See the CNBC European Business website
(http://cnceb.com/2007/03/01/the_innovation_issue/).

The follow-through imperative

One executive told us: 'You are absolutely right regarding the follow-through weaknesses of managers. This is the single most important – but also most difficult – part of our jobs.' You can delegate many managerial tasks. But you cannot delegate follow-through because it is the only process through which an organization can become better and better at what it does. Another executive explained the importance of follow-through by stating: 'You plan, you set milestones, you follow up, and you follow through. It has to be a disciplined process, not nebulous. You have to be relentless. You cannot ever say "we will let it go this time."' And, in fact, follow-through is even more critical to strategic initiatives than it is to management in general. Initiatives are not routine work. They compete with many, more or less 'routine' tasks that keep the organization fully occupied. They compete for people's time, resources and management attention.

While how to perform many other tasks in an organization is well known, this is not the case for most strategic initiatives. Initiative teams need to learn on the go, which is unusual in many organizations. Without follow-through, learning will never happen. And, while most standard tasks in an organization are performed at 'cruising altitude', strategic initiatives require a real surge of energy to be completed. There are few opportunities to sit back and rest. Follow-through helps maintain execution energy. So, there are three reasons why follow-through is most critical for the successful execution of strategic initiatives:

◆ Follow-through is imperative to keep execution on course

◆ Follow-through is imperative to learn on the go

◆ Follow-through is imperative to maintain execution energy

We'll provide our reasons for saying this as we discuss each of the three reasons.

Keeping execution on course

Execution milestones have been set. They specify the results to be achieved by certain dates for the overall execution to be successful. Milestones are commitments. Assessing that they are reached is the first purpose of follow-through. Corrective actions must then be decided promptly to get back on track if the expected milestones have not been achieved. Corrections must also be decided promptly if the results achieved show that execution could be more ambitious.

A milestone that is not reached is a milestone that is not achieved. It is not wise to move a milestone just because it was not met. A milestone that is not reached provides critical information to review; this information, if acted upon, can improve your overall execution plan. If the milestone was moved, for whatever reason, that information would be ignored. Even if a milestone turns out to be unrealistic, it should not be moved. The next milestones should incorporate corrective actions. Many feedback sessions debate at length whether a milestone needs to be moved. But the only issue that is worth debating is what needs to be done next to ensure a successful execution.

Follow-through reviews are also the time for mentally rehearsing the next moves. Follow-through ensures that the next execution steps are thoroughly mentally rehearsed. It allows the team members to be all on the same page. It maintains the necessary coordination among them. Leaving no stone unturned in preparing the next steps, raising what-if questions about what might occur, anticipating corrective actions: this is all an integral part of follow-through. Therefore, make sure that you:

Encourage open communications

Keeping the execution on course requires open communication. Good news and bad news must be brought to the surface. Team members must come forward with progress information. The best team members will, of course, have anticipated problems and acted immediately. A close second is that they asked for help when they didn't know what to do. And saying nothing is clearly the worst possible conduct; no one can solve a problem if it is denied.

In follow-through cultures, members of the execution team have the relevant progress information at their finger tips. You don't hear during review meetings: 'I *guess* we have a problem; let's study it and discuss it again next time.' The team members know exactly which questions will be discussed, what information will be expected, and they come prepared to solve problems.

In such meetings, discussions should focus on what to do next, more than on what happened, and even less on whose fault it is. No one should sweep contentious issues under the carpet. Ideally, corrective actions have already been started and the discussion moves on to the next battle, rather than the last one. In follow-through cultures 'bad news' is just data – valuable data – that can be acted upon to everyone's benefit.

Avoid communication killers

There are certain ways of running progress reviews that are true communication killers. A common one is to breed a blame culture by spending the time looking for culprits and pointing fingers. All team members will immediately run for cover. Information will no longer be surfaced. At review meetings, everyone will shut up, hoping that someone else gets scrutinized before them. When accusations come their way, they will have prepared all the excuses to deflect them. In time, team members start fighting preventively. Initiative and accountability disappear. Then, when there is a problem, people just hope that it disappears or resolves itself before it is discovered. If it is ever addressed, it will be too late.

Another effective way to kill communications is to 'kill the messengers'. Some bosses exhibit a strong resentment of bad news and effectively discourage any. Sometimes, they also take such bad news very personally, as if they were being betrayed by someone telling them the truth. If this happens to an initiative sponsor or team leader, there will be a serious problem thenceforth. Team members will refrain from annoying the boss and choose silence. Soon, there will be no bad news reported. It will be like having a party on a yacht lost in thick fog.

Of course, a frequent information killer is to have no progress review at all. Some executives, and some teams, routinely cancel these meetings. It means that there are more important things to do than monitoring the progress of the initiative. It legitimizes the view that this information is of no consequence. It is a huge mistake.

Learning on the go

Learning as you go is the second purpose of follow-through. Most strategic initiatives happen in the unknown territory of cross-organization challenges. Each team member may be an expert in one part of the challenge: new technology, new engineering, new processes, new markets and so on. Probably, no team member is an expert in every aspect of the work to be done. Most team members will be scrambling to learn as fast as possible. They will be looking for ready-made solutions and right answers. They will be visiting other companies for template approaches. All of this is good, but, in the end, the most useful learning will come from trial and error. Wise sponsors and team leaders will steer their teams as soon as possible towards rapid prototyping, debriefing and learning. Follow-through reviews provide these indispensable learning opportunities before moving forward.

In follow-through cultures, for example, 'well-thought-out mistakes' are seen as a potential source of learning. After-action reviews are conducted frequently and routinely. Best practice is documented, shared and systematically researched to guide execution. If learning is effective, these same mistakes are expected not to happen again.

If you're learning on the go, problems and setbacks are taken at face value as opportunities to learn. What matters is really what to do next. What happened is only relevant to the extent that something useful for the future can be learned from it. Pointing at problems should thus be immediately followed by proposing solutions. To achieve such a helpful state, you have to:

Encourage frequent feedback

Smart and agile execution seeks to generate very frequent feedback on intermediary deliverables, without waiting for spectacular results. For example, feedback is sought on proposals, on early prototypes, on pilots. In particular, it is sought as early as possible from the target adopters and from the customers. In that way, teams make sure they get data that will help them improve as fast as possible, before too much damage is done and too much money is spent.

Follow-through can then focus on tangible results and critical questions such as whether the initiative is making money. Otherwise, execution is only guided by proxy measures of success, such as being on time or on budget. But you may be on time and on budget with the wrong solution. By focusing early on tangible results, the team has a chance to learn and to apply its learning immediately, while there is still time to improve and money is in the budget to spend on the improvements.

Encourage people taking responsibility

A condition to learn fast is clearly to recognize that the results obtained are the outcome of one's own actions. If results were the outcome of some 'invisible hand', trying to improve would be pointless: the 'invisible hand' would always be the cause for the results. In follow-through cultures, people take responsibility for their own performance. If you care about proving yourself, you want a successful outcome to be attributed to your efforts, rather than to some other factors. Even in the case of failure, invoking excuses would mean a loss of face.

In follow-through cultures, teams also develop a self-regulated approach to their performance. Their mutual dependency makes them jointly accountable for addressing, and even anticipating, problems, whoever's lap they leap upon. 'Not my job!' is totally irrelevant for such team members. Self-regulation is a norm. Peer pressure in this instance becomes much more effective than top–down control. The boss will never know everything that is going on, but team members do and will act immediately or else everyone will suffer. They will also correct their own mistakes faster. As one executive observed: 'It is easy to fool senior management but much harder to fool your peers. They can be very blunt with each other.'

Purge learning killers

The communication killers that we have just discussed are also learning killers. Not only do they deprive the team of valuable progress information, they also suppress the chance to do better in the future. An example is the performance review that focuses on individuals rather than on what the team should do next. Another example is dwelling on the consequences of a mistake that cannot be undone, rather than on reviewing the reasoning that caused it and that can be changed in the future.

Another very effective way to kill learning is to find endless excuses. In many organizations, you only hear excuses – the summer was rainy and the winter had no snow – and it is generally someone else's fault. This happens, of course, most frequently in the case of failure. As one execution leader observed, 'There is a fine line between excuses and reasons.' Similarly, concluding that things will only improve if the other department down the hall changes its attitude is unlikely to help anyone. If the only learning point is that all current problems are someone else's fault, there is not much that can be done to apply what's been learned and improve execution.

Maintaining momentum

Maintaining the execution energy is the third purpose of follow-through. Earlier in the book, we discussed three motives that inspire your team members: ambition, thrust and team drive. Follow-through reviews provide repeated opportunities to satisfy these motives and to support the team's energy and commitment. In these ways, you can do as follows.

Support healthy ambition

Some of your team members are achievers and are energized by their ambition to push the limits. We saw earlier how important feedback was for them to maintain their energy. 'Everyone needs milestones and needs to be constantly measured on an ongoing basis. Good people even relish it,' observed one sponsor we worked with. Follow-through provides many opportunities to recognize one's performance at the same time as the team's performance is being reviewed.

Even a disappointing performance is an opportunity to boost the energy of the achievers in your team. They are keen to prove that they can perform at a high level and constructive solution-seeking is important to them – even at the cost of reviewing embarrassing results.

In some cultures, it is not customary to give positive feedback. What works well is supposed to work anyway. It is rather what doesn't work that is emphasized. We believe that a sustained recognition deficit undermines team energy while simple personal recognition goes a long way.

Maintain thrust

Teams will sometimes seek to be told what to do. This is not a sign of energy. Smart sponsors and team leaders will throw the ball back at them with guiding questions: 'What do you think? Did you think about...?'

Follow-through is the opportunity to put execution back in the hands of your execution team. Challenge the team's thinking to make it more robust. In time, team members will make sure that the team reviews its next steps thoroughly as often as they can. To allow this to happen, however, review meetings must not be run as detective inquiries on the team's performance. Challenging the team to perform its own inquiry and reach its own conclusions will be an effective way to stimulate the energy of the whole team.

Consistency of follow-through is also necessary. The same points that were discussed at the last review should again be noted at the next one. The same priorities should be emphasized, time and again, review after review. If the rules of the game are constantly changed, the team's energy will soon evaporate.

Boost team drive

Follow-through makes the team members aware of their mutual dependency in delivering results. They can't help but realize how much they depend on each other's performance. With your support, team members will see that mutual support is their best next step. The energy will increase. It will help everyone understand that they are also jointly accountable. The team members become more demanding with each other and energy increases even more.

Follow-through is also an opportunity for you to monitor how the team works. There are few more demoralizing scenes than a poorly functioning team. You sense the thickness of the air as soon as you walk into the room where the dysfunctional team is meeting. You don't feel very welcome. Some team members stand aloof from the rest. Follow-through encounters, such as review meetings, or impromptu occasions, will soon reveal such problems. There will be obvious and subtle signals of conflicts.

In a high-performance team, conflicts are natural. They result from the high-performance drive of team members. They are exacerbated by the pressure on the entire team to deliver results. The problem is not that there is a conflict. The real problem is not knowing how to get out of it. Those at the origin of the conflict are embarrassed for having created it and perhaps for having burst out. And everyone else suffers.

It can be tempting to sweep conflict issues under the carpet and to move on, 'as mature adults'. This approach just consumes more energy. The issues will resurface. So, whenever a conflict arises, effective teams address it immediately.

It is not about what happened (which will soon be forgotten anyway), but about the bad memories and emotions it triggers. If they are not addressed, the same negatively connoted emotions will come back with different causes anyway.

In fact, even if the conflict seems to be between only two persons, every team member has something on their heart. So, every team member needs the chance to state their concerns and issues. These need to be addressed as a team, agreeing on how best to remove them and on what to do to make sure that the same issues don't repeat themselves. This may require the skilful support of the team leader and, in some cases, of the sponsor. But it can be a bonding experience for a team. It will raise its confidence in its ability to manage itself. As a result, the team will come out of it with more energy.

Support commitment

Follow-through also provides you with the opportunity to exemplify the behaviours you expect from the team to support execution. You must make your mode of interaction visibly focused on progressing. You can demonstrate that you prioritize discussing future steps over deciphering what happened. You can make it very clear that you are not interested in whose fault it is, but on what to do next. In doing so, you prove that you are genuinely interested in the success of the team in carrying out the initiative.

While follow-through most naturally focuses on the work of the team, it is also about providing genuine attention to individual team members. Follow-through yields substantial information about the motives of every team member. You see how each team member responds under pressure. You see how each team member handles failures. You see what makes each one click. You see which individual actions feed the team's energy. For a leader, and for any team member, this is essential information to help the team progress and to make energy contagious.

Follow-through is an opportunity to demonstrate this personal attention, either during review meetings or on other occasions. Showing a personal concern for individuals, for their families or for their personal projects, is an integral part of follow-through.

And remember how easy it is to sap commitment

No follow-through or bad follow-through are very effective ways to kill commitment. It starts with denying people feedback, as if performance, good or bad, made no difference. Many people have themselves experienced receiving lip-service feedback and been perplexed by it. No feedback on a performance that is known to be below par is even more demoralizing to high-achievers. No recognition of high performance can be very demoralizing also, particularly when someone else steals the glory. Sponsors who would manage to get all the visibility for themselves without ever sharing the success with the team will soon be let down by the team.

Similarly, running review meetings mostly in a top–down style may infuse discipline but kill the energy. If the team senses that its only option is to do what it was told to do there will not be much motivation – either to do it, or even less to respond to difficulties and setbacks in the execution.

Finally, lack of consistency in follow-through is also a way to kill commitment. Some senior managers can be remarkably unsystematic in their performance monitoring. For example, they react beyond reason to the latest event, while forgetting what was agreed at the last review. Or they impose schizophrenic demands, whereby people can be caught on the wrong foot whatever they do. Or they put their team at the mercy of whimsical verdicts. This will undermine self-respect and sap any commitment.

Implementing follow-through

There are many follow-through occasions. Team leaders, who spend a lot of time with their team, should have no difficulty creating and leveraging such occasions. It requires more of a special effort from the initiative sponsors. They are not with the team all the time, and it is easier for them to let their attention drift away. But *occasional* follow-through is not *true* follow-through. Continuity of follow-through is essential. To ensure continuous follow-through, we recommend two complementary meetings: operating review meetings and milestone meetings. But, as you will read, continuous follow-through also calls for action between meetings.

Operating-review meetings

Operating-review meetings are the regular team meetings held by the team leader and attended by the team. The regularity of the meetings creates the 'heartbeat' of the project. These meetings pump oxygen into the team and create the energy needed for the team to keep going. Without regularity, the team members will easily forget the initiative. 'Out of sight' rapidly becomes 'out of mind'. With regularity, the team will feel that the initiative remains top priority. These meetings build stamina and increase the ability of the team to execute, much in the same way that regular exercise builds fitness.

Sure, there will be days when the last thing you need on your agenda is the project meeting – and even other times when there is really nothing to say. No matter. *It is critical to meet anyway.* An expert team coach told us that, in her opinion, the ability of the team to stick to these regular meetings is her biggest predictor of team success.

Operating-review meetings must be led by the team leader. Here are some practical suggestions for running these meetings.

Who should attend the operating-review meetings?

The meeting must be attended by all the team members. You might also include members of the extended team at various key points or for meetings that lead up to important milestones. But keep the number of people manageable. With more than 10 people, discussions are going to be slow and cumbersome.

If you have decided to work closely together with the sponsor to lead the team, then the sponsor will also join these meetings on a regular basis. Even if you are responsible for the day-to-day running of the team, the sponsor should attend from time to time. It is a good opportunity for him to see how the team is doing, or to provide some coaching or simply to raise team morale.

Team members should be under no illusions; attendance is not optional. If a team member cannot attend, you must insist that she let the rest of the team know as far in advance as possible. She needs to send her progress update to the other team members *before* the meeting takes place. If a team member is missing without warning, you should contact him as soon as possible after the meeting to discuss his absence and ask him to send his progress update to the team immediately. Frequent unexplained absences should be discussed during norm reviews and, if appropriate, the team can choose to introduce a penalty system with, for example, donations to charity.

What should be the frequency and duration of operating-review meetings?

A strategic-initiative team should meet every week or every second week. This choice depends partly on the nature of the initiative: 'short sprint' initiatives require weekly meetings; 'long distance' initiatives may work fine with bi-weekly meetings. It also depends on how well the team members know each other and how confident they are in working together. Teams with lower confidence should meet more often.

The key is to plan these meetings well in advance. Before execution gets under way, the dates and times of each operating-review meeting for the duration of the initiative must be scheduled in advance. It may sound a little stupid to plan meetings so far ahead but, once you have planned the meetings, then it requires active effort on behalf of the team to remove the dates from their diaries, making the meetings much harder to cancel.

Typically, these meetings should be relatively short. For teams that meet face to face, then two to three hours should be the maximum. This is about the right duration; any longer, and you will reach the limit of people's attention span. If these meetings drag on longer than scheduled, then this is a sign that they are not run effectively. Another important rule is that all meetings should start and end on schedule; this way nobody wastes their time.

What should the agenda of operating-review meetings be?

Typically, it is best to have a standard agenda for these meetings. The team members will know what to expect and the meetings will be more efficient. Although it is important to follow the timetable, it is also important to set aside enough time for discussion and also for some personal sharing and human contact. A typical agenda might comprise the following items.

Review what the team has completed since the last meeting

At the start of the meeting, ask each of the team members to present the actions completed since the last meeting. With seven team members, each team member needs to keep his description relatively short. A one-page performance tracker (with the decisions made at the previous review, the expected results, the actual results and proposed next steps) helps to keep everyone focused. You must encourage the other team members to ask questions by clarifying points and flagging potential difficulties that they see ahead.

Review issues that have arisen

As you listen to these reports, ask the team to focus on the parts of the execution roadmap that are not on track. For each of the issues, while encouraging supportive challenge, ask the person responsible for the task what the underlying root causes are. Ask the person to propose corrective actions. If needed, get the whole team to work on these corrective actions. Find out where the person needs help. Then, get the team to agree on the solution and the next steps.

Discuss the next steps

Now, review with the team the next steps in the execution roadmap. Each team member must explain what they intend to do. Providing supportive challenge, encourage the team to mentally rehearse its next steps. Make sure that a full description of the deliverables and deadlines is provided. Review with the team any special difficulties with upcoming tasks. Review the execution risks that may come into play. Agree with the team on how to monitor these risks and on any contingency plans that a team member may need to activate.

Summarize decisions

At the end of the meeting, review the key decisions made along with deadlines and responsibilities. Minutes of the meeting should also be circulated shortly after the meeting ends, within hours – certainly, within 24 hours.

Milestone meetings

These meetings take a broader perspective than the operating-review meetings. They are used to look at progress in the broader context of the overall initiative and of the strategy. They take place at the time of the most important execution milestones (per the overall schedule of the strategic initiative), specifically when closure of one stage of progress is required before moving on, or when critical decisions have to be made to steer the next few execution phases. Milestone meetings are typically led by the initiative sponsor.

Milestone meetings could combine several of the following purposes in one meeting, or address them separately. Sometimes, they may mix well in one single meeting; sometimes different milestone meetings may be required.

Launching a critical execution phase

Two outcomes may be sought with these meetings. One is to boost the execution energy of the team just before starting an important phase. The other is to reinforce the commitment of the extended team that will contribute, along with the core team, to this next phase.

After the team has worked with its target adopters and suppliers of resources to prepare its execution plan, it can now be presented here. There should be no surprises in it for the sponsor. The sponsor must have worked with the team leader and possibly with the team in such a way that it does not have to be turned down at the milestone meeting.

However, this does not preclude further probing of the robustness of the plan at the milestone meeting, possibly involving a wider audience. This will give the sponsor an important opportunity to signal that everyone's commitment is expected. Of course, it is also an opportunity to signal the strong commitment of the sponsor herself. If other members of the top management team have been invited to the meeting, their commitment is also an important requisite for the team to feel encouraged.

Closing an important execution phase

These milestone meetings will usually include at least one after-action review (see opposite). The purpose is to extract the learning points from the phase that has been completed and to outline possible options for moving forward.

A wider audience, to whom these learning points are relevant, can be invited to these milestone meetings. Typically, this will be the case with the

After-Action Review

After-action review (AAR) is a continuous-improvement and learning procedure routinely practised in some contexts, especially when learning is vital. For example, it has long been part of military procedures in many countries. But it is relatively less practised in corporate contexts. AAR consists of four steps:

1   What is the variance – positive or negative – between the objectives of the project and the results actually achieved?

2   What was the chronology of events – project execution steps – that led to the actual results?

   ◆   At each step in the chronology, what was the expected outcome and what was the actual outcome?

   ◆   What happened that led to a variance?

   ◆   Causes may have to do, for example, with people, resources, processes, infrastructure. Which?

3   What were the most important causes that led to the overall variance?

   ◆   Recurring causes, big-impact causes, wider-organization causes?

4   What are the key learning points that you can draw from the AAR?

   ◆   What must be done to be more successful in the future?

   ◆   To whom must these learning points be communicated? How? When?

Six important rules must be respected by those involved in an AAR:

◆   *No blaming: focus on actions more than on their authors*

◆   *Everyone participates: all perspectives are required*

◆   *Absolute honesty: nothing is swept under the carpet*

◆   *No thin skins: no emotional outburst*

◆   *Stick to the facts: refer to facts, not to opinions*

◆   *No retribution: ever*

extended-team members who have participated in that phase – for example, the target adopters who have been involved in a pilot will need to be included.

It is also possible that other teams who are involved in parallel initiatives are asked to participate in these milestone meetings. They may share their own learning points and complement the team's perspective.

Choosing among future options

Smart and agile execution provides frequent decision points on how to move forward. The most important of these decision points require milestone meetings.

They require from the sponsor a thorough preparation with the team leader, and possibly with the team, long before the milestone meeting. It would not be responsible to wait until then to start thinking about the issue. Before the meeting, the sponsor must have already gained a reasonably established view of how to proceed. These decisions need to be made promptly and transparently in order to maintain the team's energy.

Normally, the team will make a recommendation that already has the sponsor's implicit support. Other executives attending, and possibly involved in the decision, must have been briefed. But even if there is no surprise, the opportunity for the team to present its proposal to such an audience will reinforce its own commitment. It will also give it more legitimacy to pursue its execution drive.

In some instances, the team and the sponsor may disagree. This may happen in a go/no-go decision. The decision must be made transparently and without delay. The sponsor will have to say 'no', and explain to the team why it is 'no', looking team members in the eyes. A no-go decision can be painful. But involving the team in it, in preparation for the meeting and at the meeting, will retain its motivation for later initiatives.

These kinds of decision-milestone meetings are an integral part of smart and agile execution. They are successful when they boost the team's energy – and we have seen occasions when they can also kill team energy very fast. Success clearly depends on the amount of preparation the sponsor and the other involved senior executives have put in. They must come to these meetings sufficiently prepared to feel comfortable with making their decisions transparently and rapidly, preferably before the end of the meeting.

Celebrating the team's progress

These milestone meetings are more likely to be energy boosters. In fact, this is their very purpose. There are different ways in which a team may get recognition for its achievements. In some cultures, just a public 'thank you' is sufficient.

Another effective form of recognition is to ask the team to present its achievements to a wider audience. Senior management meetings can provide such opportunities. Most companies also have a yearly convention of their managers above a certain level. These occasions provide the necessary visibility to work as incentives.

In some instances, the sponsor may choose to resort to less public rewards. For example, sponsoring a weekend with the team members' families may be a recognition for the personal sacrifices they have made because of the initiative.

Keeping the finger on the pulse

Follow-through doesn't stop at the end of the operating-review meeting or of the milestone meeting. In fact, outside these formal occasions, there is always the risk that the initiative becomes de-prioritized. The meter starts ticking again for the 'day jobs' of the team members. But these periods of time also provide the sponsor and the team leader with numerous opportunities to gather useful progress information and to steer execution. Follow-through requires that you keep a finger on the pulse of the initiative, to determine whether it is in good health. Here are four ways you can continue to follow through, outside a formal context like an operating-review meeting or a milestone meeting.

Lead from the front

Some managers position themselves as 'hands-off leaders' as if it was the latest leadership theory. Under the pretext of not micromanaging, they are never around to provide guidance or simply a reassuring presence. They simply do not know what is going on.

Some initiative sponsors, and even some team leaders, disappear between review meetings. Like seagulls, they fly in for the review, make a noise, and fly out. They seem to believe that it is enough just to tell someone to do something. Then their own job is done until the next follow-up point when they will check the results – if they have not forgotten what they said. Talk about an energy killer.

In follow-through cultures, the sponsor and the team leader keep their finger on the pulse of execution. They have the capability to be present without interfering with individual responsibilities. One sponsor noted: 'It is hard to know when to interfere. Sometimes you don't catch things fast enough, or you let them last longer than you should. There is no real sign when you should interfere. In fact, there are signs all along the way, but it is still a judgement call when to get involved. It depends on how perceptive you are. Some people are better at this than others.'

The sponsor, in particular, may be more distant from the team; thus, he must do his best to remain visible and reachable. An effective sponsor makes it clear to the team members that, when it is about the initiative, he is more than happy to be 'disturbed'. Such sponsors give instructions to that effect to their assistants.

Gather progress information

The sponsor is not only available to answer questions. In follow-through cultures, the sponsor and the team leader use every opportunity to gather information on execution progress.

They make sure they encounter individual team members and ask questions about how they see the initiative progressing. Reading between the lines of responses, they can get a feel for what is going on in different parts of the initiative. They can sense what the team's level of energy is.

They also use impromptu meetings – in the corridors, in the lifts, at the cafeteria – to gather progress information from team members. By providing fast responses when a team member has questions or raises issues in impromptu encounters, they demonstrate their desire to listen and be informed: 'Let's talk about this right now; come down to my office.' And they create opportunities to obtain even more progress information, while remaining informal.

They also talk to other people in the organization to get a sense of how the initiative is doing. They solicit feedback on the execution. One sponsor noted: 'Typically, people are not deliberately misleading you. But they may be either unaware or fooling themselves. I normally go and speak personally to the people who have to do the execution to find out whether there is a need for a wake-up call.'

Pick up weak signals

The purpose of all this informal information gathering is to allow the team leader, but, more importantly, the sponsor, to play a role that they, alone, can play because of their experience: spotting weak signals, before the team has the problem.

An experienced sponsor has a sense for picking up these weak signals and for linking the dots. She can see future issues and challenges brewing before they become too large to manage quickly. Intervening with the team is always a judgement call. Teams benefit when they can solve their own problems. Sometimes, however, a sponsor's involvement can save time, minimize damage, and help the team learn – all at once. But this will only occur if the sponsor is tuning in to the weak signals of distress that may be coming from the team.

Weak signals may be picked up anywhere and spotting them is a matter of experience. But how the team is working is worth monitoring all the time. As discussed earlier, this can be one of the most damaging issues, if left unaddressed. These are issues that most teams will hesitate to bring up. Even team leaders will avoid admitting to their sponsor that two team members don't seem to be able to work with each other, or that they cannot handle a difficult team member. Signs like the effectiveness of discussions, the ability to reach a closure, the lack of involvement of a team member, will all give clues to the sensitive sponsor. From the beginning, the sponsor should get the team accustomed to his silent presence during some of their meetings so that it is perceived as normal. This is a very effective way for a sponsor to perceive the subtle signals of fermenting team issues.

Steer the team

The sponsor has unique opportunities, outside formal occasions, to send signals to the team on what matters. Precisely because these are outside the sponsor's formal role, the team will pay much attention to the sponsor's informal behaviour and attitude towards the initiative.

Unfortunately, in these informal instances, the sponsor also has a signifi-cant possibility to demotivate the team and to reduce its execution energy. When the team can observe a clear lack of consistency between what the sponsor said during the milestone meetings, and what the sponsor does the rest of the time, their energy will suffer. A sponsor must be credible at all times.

When, in informal encounters, no questions are asked, or, even worse, when emphatic congratulations are dispensed to a team member who knows that progress is (in fact) quite slow, people will doubt that the initiative is really uppermost in the sponsor's mind. When a concerned team member volunteers her worries to the sponsor, then hears a response of 'Let's talk about it at the next meeting', she will have to conclude that the initiative is not a real priority.

What the team is looking for, to decide whether the sponsor is serious, is continuity across formal *and* informal encounters. Every-day behaviours and attitudes – knowing what is going on, asking the right questions, responding without delay, going out of one's way to be informed – are more convincing than formal speeches.

One sponsor we met put it this way: 'If you follow a process long enough, it becomes ingrained and leads to culture. You have to be consistent with the process.' This should be your ambition: to develop in your organization *a follow-through culture*. To a certain extent, such an achievement is a matter of establishing firm, effective, constructive processes. They provide the beat of a follow-through culture. But, to a much larger extent, a follow-through culture comes from the relentless attention, first, of every sponsor of new strategic initiatives – and of every other senior executive in your organization.

Make sure you never forget that follow-through is more than a process; *it is hands-on leadership*.

Epilogue:
A double-edged strategy

'However beautiful the strategy,' Winston Churchill said, with a knowing gleam in his eye, 'you should occasionally look at the results.' Churchill was probably talking about statecraft at the time, not business management, but his words ring equally true to us. It has been our goal, via this book, to raise attention to the double-edged nature of strategy. On the one hand, strategy is a major responsibility of senior managers, one that can be exciting and possibly even revolutionary. Thus, we understand and salute all the marvellous accolades bestowed upon strategic leaders around the world by media and academic authorities who focus intently on the making of a strategic vision. However, too often, those same authorities don't look at the results; they forget that (in the words of an anonymous commentator): *strategy gets you on the playing field, but execution pays the bills.* Thus, on the other hand, strategic vision carries huge inherent risk.

You may not have heard the name of Guy Kawasaki, although everyone now knows the name of Steve Jobs. Both gentlemen were involved in the early days at Apple Computer, Jobs as CEO and Kawasaki as a leader in Apple's marketing and product innovation divisions. That was back in the 1980s, but we recently caught this 2007 observation by Kawasaki:

> *This is what I call the strategy paradox. That is, the same strategies that have the highest probability of extreme success also have the highest probability of extreme failure. In other words, everything we know about the linkage between strategy and success is true, but dangerously*

incomplete. Vision, commitment, focus ... these are all in fact the defining elements of successful strategies, but they are also systematically connected with some of the greatest strategic disasters.[1]

We found Kawasaki's words most powerful and thus chose to close our book with them, because we think we know exactly what he's talking about. In company after company, we have seen brilliant initiatives launched with confidence and fanfare. In most of them, regrettably, the brilliance was never backed up with execution. Thus, as Kawasaki states, the greater the strategic leap, the greater the risk that – without thorough and painstaking execution – success will devolve into mediocrity, if not abject failure.

Time and again, we have seen experienced corporate managers fall prey to a bad selection of strategic initiatives, so that any option they deployed was doomed from the start. Then, too, we have seen a great strategic idea handed over to a suboptimal team, crippling the chance for the initiative to achieve its promise. We've sat with top managers who suffered from a clear-cut case of muddled scope, of sagging spirit, of a penchant for improvisation more than a talent for execution: in all such cases, the strategic initiative they gave birth to never grew to a mature success.

And we would not have to search our files (or our memories) very long to find cases of great managers launching great initiatives *without any care* whether the people in the organizations they led were on board for this adventure. And we have seen charming, personable managers who – after solidly allocating resources and launching a new initiative – became reclusive or preoccupied with other matters, leaving the strategic initiative's execution team to wonder whether they were pioneers in charting a new corporate destiny or outcasts no longer welcome in the executive suites that mandated their work. In other words, we have seen corporate leaders who never learned that they themselves must follow through or risk the failure of their own strategic initiative.

We wrote this book with the profound hope that you would find here seven insights to overcome the seven execution challenges we summarized above. These are the same seven challenges profiled in our Introduction, which link to the seven main chapters of this book. *Execution* has been, for the last few years, the watchword of the business world. It only makes sense.

---

[1] HighContrast: Innovation & venture capital in the post-broadband era (Simeon Simeonov's weblog: http://simeons.wordpress.com/2007/02/21/guy-kawasaki-why-good-strategies-fail/).

Lots of companies are trying many new things. New products and new services abound. But sloppy execution is what we see in most companies, and thus we press every corporate leader we meet to commit himself to *smarter* execution. For, in the final analysis, overcoming the barriers to success begins with developing your own abilities to take a great business idea, to work *with* others to bring it to life, and to follow its execution through *to full completion*.

In a fast-changing world, execution *is* strategic thinking.

Index